The Sea Kayaker's Guide to Mount Desert Island

The Sea Kayaker's
GUIDE

to Mount Desert Island

Jennifer Alisa Paigen

Illustrations and Charts by **Karen Svenson**

Photographs by **W. David Andrews II**

Down East Books

COPYRIGHT © 1997 BY JENNIFER ALISA PAIGEN

ISBN 0-089272-380-7

BOOK DESIGN BY LURELLE CHEVERIE

Color separation by Roxmont Graphics

Printed and bound at BookCrafters, Inc.

5   4   3

DOWN EAST BOOKS / CAMDEN, MAINE

LIBRARY OF CONGRESS CATALOGING-IN PUBLICATION DATA

Paigen, Jennifer Alisa, 1971–

    The sea kayaker's guide to Mount Desert Island / by Jennifer Alisa Paigen.

       p.   cm.

    Includes bibliographical references (p.).

    ISBN 0-89272-380-7

    1. Sea kayaking—Maine—Mount Desert Island—Guidebooks.   2. Mount Desert Island (Me.)—Guidebooks.   I. Title.

    GV776.M22M686 1997

    797.1'22'0974145—dc21

97-6534

CIP

TO ALL THOSE COMMITTED TO THE FREEDOM OF

EXPERIENTIAL EDUCATION.

MAY THIS BOOK BE A CELEBRATION AND EXAMPLE OF

THE ACCOMPLISHMENTS THAT CAN

COME FROM STUDENT-DIRECTED LEARNING.

Contents

Acknowledgments

So many people have helped create this book over the last few years. I believe strongly in giving back to those who gave to me, and so let me say thank you to the following people. I appreciate all your help:

Several members of the Hampshire College faculty, staff, and alumni have been instrumental in this project's development: David Smith, in the School of Humanities and Arts; Ken Hoffman, in the School of Natural Sciences; Will Ryan, in the Writing Program; Alesia Maltz (Class F74); Eric Pinder (Class F88); Chris Chase, in the School of Communication and Cognitive Sciences; and John Reid, in the School of Natural Sciences.

Many field experts critiqued drafts, including: Forrest Dillon, of Maine Coast Heritage Trust; Angela Matz, at the University of Maine (Orono); Leslie Cowperthwaite, Maine Seal; John Anderson, at College of the Atlantic; Frank Matter, Acadia Publishing; and David Manski and Charles Jacobi, Acadia National Park.

I also wish to thank W. David Andrews II for making his prolific photography talent available, and Karen Svenson for providing the beautiful and timely illustrations and charts. For keeping me employed and assisting with logistics throughout, I thank the staff at Coastal Kayaking: Cliff VandenBosch, Marty Lloyd, Joe Dunn, and Eric Bruner.

Thanks are also due to all the guides that I have worked with over the years, including (though certainly not limited to): Ron Wanner, Drew Maples, Tim Coffren, Armand Michaud, Chris Kelly, Angie Delvecchio, Natalie Springuel, Bob DeForrest, Jenny Cohen, Kris Recklifs, Chuck Herrick, Adam Wales, Dan Liden, Shane Dugan, and Oliver Waldman. Each of you taught me something that I was able to use in this book.

Finally, I would like to thank my parents, Beverly and Kenneth Paigen: when I was a child, you showed me the wonders of Mount Desert Island and taught me to seek adventure; during my student years, you gave me the freedom to learn and explore. As an adult, I look to your example of how to be a true scientist, naturalist, and teacher. You have supported me through all my goals with unconditional love and endless editing. I only hope that I can give the same gifts to my children and students.

The sea that calls all things unto her
calls me, and I must embark.

KAHLIL GIBRAN, *THE PROPHET*

INTRODUCTION

A Sense of Time and Space

All the islands are different;
all have their particular meaning.
This one is a sanctuary
for the wild places of the soul.
—**PHILIP CONKLING**

While Philip Conkling was writing of one particular Maine island, "this one" could easily refer to Mount Desert or any other Maine island. Once you have an island underfoot, your outlook is forever changed.

Islands are distinctly individual, each having its own personality, each a unique gem in a sea of wealth. What is it that draws us to these mountaintops in the sea? What is their magical quality that awakens our soul? The answers are as individual as the islands themselves.

As the gull flies, the coast of Maine extends only 250 miles—quite a short trip for so much beauty. Following the shoreline, each and every bay and inlet, the trip would be 2,500 miles long, and traveling every true shore-mile, incorporating islands and all, the trip would be over 3,750 enjoyable miles. The most striking characteristic of this coast is its abundance of islands—three thousand of them—more than lie along the rest of the entire eastern seaboard.

Maine's highest mountaintop of the sea, Mount Desert Island, is home to unparalleled beauty, much of which is protected as part of Acadia National Park. "Acadia had its charms, and it has them still," wrote one enraptured soul, "in its wilderness of woods and its wilderness of waves; . . . [and in] the romantic highlands of Mount Desert, down whose gorges the sea-fog rolls like an invading host, while the spires of fir-trees pierce the surging vapors like lances in the smoke of battle." (Samuel Drake, *The Pine Tree Coast*, 1891.)

As a child growing up on Mount Desert, I spent most of my summers exploring and playing among the wonders of the island. I gathered wild edibles from the seashore, spent countless hours staring into tidepools, and developed an undying love for this area—a passion that runs deep within my soul.

In the summer of 1989 my family became year-round residents, and I was hired as a sea kayaking guide by a local outfitter. I found, after spending days and days out on the water, that I wanted to go beyond simply enjoyment; I wanted to develop understanding and knowledge. I felt that to enter a world knowing little about it was to enter a vacuum. To experience without understanding is like viewing the world through a fogged pane of glass, never fully understanding what is seen and lacking the ability to appreciate its beauty.

As I studied and observed, I began to perceive even more of the Maine coast's magnificent beauty and to deepen my understanding of my role as a kayaker in the waters around Mount Desert Island. I truly gained a sense of time and place. It is my hope that THE SEA KAYAKER'S GUIDE TO MOUNT DESERT ISLAND will be more than a simple guidebook. It is a tool designed to help you on your own path of discovery.

Practical advice forms the backbone of any guidebook, and my primary purpose is to provide you with the necessary practical information to embark upon a safe and enjoyable paddling adventure. I know from first-hand experience how important this is. One recent trip serves as a good example.

It was a sunny day in early April. Out on Frenchman Bay, the sun sparkled brighter than I remembered ever seeing before. Eager to paddle again after a long winter, I convinced a good friend to explore the Porcupine Islands with me. Gathering appropriate cold-weather gear, Kris and I paddled out into a morning that was cold but beautifully clear. A few hours later, as we sat drinking hot cocoa on Rum Key, we noticed the first signs of a winter storm off to the north. Immediately we headed back, but in a matter of minutes we were struggling against a wind so strong that it blew the froth tops off the whitecaps. It took us two and a half hours to cover the two miles back to Bar Harbor—a trip I've often completed in just thirty minutes. The storm continued for three days.

It was a humbling experience.

The sea kayak, a craft of ancient design, quiet and unobtrusive, allows the paddler to float along the edges of the aquatic and terrestrial worlds. Today this wonderful sport is being discovered by many people who, unfortunately, do not recognize its dangers or take the time to learn the required skills. The dangers of sea kayaking are subtle, but the consequences can be severe. The number of rescues along the Maine coast increases with each summer season. One local guide said to me recently, "Only in recent years have I seen more and more paddlers less prepared than ever."

> *THIS GUIDE ASSUMES THAT, BEFORE DEPARTING, YOU HAVE ALREADY MASTERED THE NEEDED SKILLS, INCLUDING CHART AND COMPASS READING, NAVIGATION, SELF-RESCUES, AND FIRST AID.*

This book is also intended as a guide for exploring the natural world. A few summers ago, naturalists (and paddlers) in this area were closely observing a pair of bald eagles to see whether they would successfully fledge any young. I was one devoted watcher and spent the majority of

Boats near Northeast Harbor, early 1900s.
NORTHEAST HARBOR LIBRARY.

my paddling time sitting a good distance away, watching the nest and birds through my binoculars. Many of my kayaking friends also got involved, and we compared notes daily.

By the end of May, I knew the eagles were indeed rearing an active and vocal chick. Not until later did I learn how truly special this birth was; this pair of eagles had not successfully hatched any chicks for several years. By the end of July, I could see the little one's head moving about. In early August, the chick began to fledge and test its wings. Finally, on an appropriately beautiful sunny day, I watched it fly straight out from the island over the open sea.

Watching an animal in the wild grow and gain its independence changed my view of the natural world. No longer were my adventures and discoveries linked to a single day or occurrence. I had seen an important milestone in one young eagle's life, and understood this bird's place within larger ecological circles. An understanding of past processes and events—geological, ecological, and historical—adds depth to our experience of the present and our role in the future.

The final purpose of this book is to provide guidelines for minimum-impact kayaking. I hope that it will encourage all paddlers to feel a sense of responsibility—of stewardship—for these waters and all their inhabitants. It was an experience several summers ago that made me realize that we can only be effective stewards of the Earth if we first gain the necessary knowledge.

One day, a group of us on our way to eat lunch on an island passed a baby seal sitting on a rock at the water's edge. With our minds focused on food, we hadn't thought much about our proximity to the young seal bellowing to its mother swimming just offshore. Eventually we left, again passing only five or ten feet away from the seal pup. Only later did I learn that our presence must have been extremely stressful for that young seal and its mother. I now know that kayakers must be aware of special environmental concerns and guidelines, and some of these are not obvious or commonly known.

THE SEA KAYAKER'S GUIDE TO MOUNT DESERT ISLAND has been organized to be useful to both the experienced naturalist and the beginner, and is designed to be brought along in a chart bag. Following a brief discussion on the local paddling conditions, the trip descriptions provide necessary safety information and trace the present natural history. The subject chapters review the Mount Desert area's past in greater depth, and the last chapter, Environmental Kayaking, concludes with minimum-impact guidelines for both land and water, and an explanation of appropriate behavior around wildlife.

I wish you good weather and safe traveling as you embark upon a journey to develop your own personal sense of time and place.

Happy paddling.

How to Use This Book

The most effective use of this guide depends on your personal learning style. I consider minimum-impact kayaking to be a necessary skill and recommend that you read that section of the book before departure. The trip summaries are most useful for reference during your excursions. Some might prefer to read the subject chapters before embarking on a paddle, while others will refer to them later. Throughout the paddling trip descriptions I include cross-references to subject chapters when appropriate.

Note that the routes described in this guide are for day trips only. Camping on islands is permitted only on state-owned islands, or on privately owned islands when you have permission from the landowners. Certain islands in the Maine Island Trail network are available for overnight use by Maine Island Trail Association members only.

The paddling conditions described in this guide are based on summer weather patterns. Fall conditions can be quite similar to summer, but winter and spring are very different and require extra caution.

Distances are given in nautical miles, unless noted otherwise.

CHARTS NEEDED FOR THIS AREA ARE:

NOAA #13318,
  Frenchman Bay and Mount Desert Island at 1:40,000.
NOAA #13316,
  Blue Hill Bay at 1:40,000.
NOAA #13312,
  Frenchman and Blue Hill Bays and approaches at 1:80,000.

DIFFICULTY LEVELS

The trips have been rated according to required skill levels.

INEXPERIENCED. People who have never paddled a kayak before or who have kayaked only on fresh water and possess only basic kayaking skills. None of the trips described in this book are appropriate for new kayakers, but there are options available, including a number of companies in Bar Harbor that offer tours led by Registered Maine Guides, as well as workshops, private lessons, and more advanced trips. The local YMCA also offers occasional workshops.

BEGINNER. The paddler possesses a working knowledge of chart and compass, navigation, rescues, and basic sea kayaking skills and has made several previous ocean kayaking trips.

INTERMEDIATE. The paddler has made full-day trips under a variety of conditions along different types of shoreline and can comfortably navigate in fog.

ADVANCED. The paddler can reliably execute an Eskimo-roll and advanced rescue techniques. Advanced paddlers have accomplished multi-day excursions and are comfortable in all coastal conditions, including high winds, large seas, and surf.

BEGINNER TRIPS: Shore Route; Mount Desert Narrows; Bartlett Narrows.

BEGINNER/INTERMEDIATE TRIPS: Seal Cove; Inner Cranberry Islands; Lower Somes Sound.

INTERMEDIATE TRIPS: The Porcupines; Bartlett Island; Upper Somes Sound.

ADVANCED ONLY TRIPS: Ironbound Island; Outer Cranberry Islands.

WIND AND WEATHER CONDITIONS

LIGHT WINDS—0 to 10 knots.
MODERATE WINDS—10 to 15 knots.
STRONG WINDS—15+ knots.

LIGHT WINDS: All paddling trips described here are possible in light wind conditions.

MODERATE WINDS: Shore Route, The Porcupines, Mount Desert Narrows, Bartlett Narrows, Bartlett Island, Seal Cove, Outer Cranberry Islands (inner harbor trip only), Inner Cranberry Islands, Lower Somes Sound, Upper Somes Sound.

STRONG WINDS: Shore Route, Mount Desert Narrows, Bartlett Narrows.

SOUTHWEST WINDS (prevailing direction in summer): All paddling trips.

NORTHWEST WINDS (usually stronger than southwest winds): Shore Route, Bartlett Narrows, Seal Cove, Inner Cranberry Islands, Outer Cranberry Islands, Lower Somes Sound, Upper Somes Sound (in lighter northwest winds).

EAST WINDS: Stay off the water. Winds from the northeast, east, or southeast are usually storm winds.

FOGGY CONDITIONS: Shore Route, Mount Desert Narrows, Bartlett Narrows, Bartlett Island, Seal Cove, Upper Somes Sound.

Local Paddling Information

This chapter is not intended to teach kayaking skills (I have included several good books on basic and advanced kayaking skills in the bibliography). Rather, it provides information on local conditions, including tides, winds and weather, and fog. Proper water and land etiquette are also discussed.

The Maine coast is not particularly forgiving, and, in general, is considered intermediate to advanced kayaking territory. It is important to be realistic about your paddling skills. This area is known for its variable weather, dense fog, substantial tides, and cold water temperatures.

In this guide I have included three beginner trips situated close to shore and in protected areas. There are also many local options for guided trips and workshops for paddlers of all skill levels.

A list of local emergency numbers is provided in Appendix A. Always leave your paddling itinerary with a friend, hotel/motel owner, or local outfitter.

TIDES

Tides are a planetary clock by which to live.
—**WILLIAM AND STEPHEN AMOS**

For any coastal residents, humans included, tides are the measure of time. For marine organisms, tides dictate reproduction, birth, feeding, and death. For the paddler, tides dictate departure and arrival, destination, and speed of travel.

Tides are caused by the gravitational pull of the sun and moon. As the moon pulls on the earth, two high tides occur, one on the side of the earth closest to the moon, the other on the side farthest away. Low tide occurs at the two locations in between. The cycle takes approximately twenty-four hours and fifty minutes, resulting in two high tides and two low tides occurring fifty minutes later each day.

moon
○

earth ◐

◌

Neap tide

Sun

tides
low → high
○ ◉→ ○

Spring tide

The sun also plays a role. When the sun is in line with the moon or directly opposite during the full and new moon, the combined gravitational pull is the strongest, resulting in exceptionally high and low tide levels—the spring tide. When the sun and moon oppose each other at right angles during the first and third quarters of the moon, the tide range is minimal—the neap tide.

In Maine, the tidal range is large, and in many places tidal currents can be strong. Tides range from an average of nine feet in Kittery to twelve feet in Bar Harbor, twenty feet in Calais, and up to fifty feet in the Bay of Fundy. The coastal Maine paddler must have a clear understanding of nature's timepiece.

To find out the time and height of Mount Desert Island tides, you should consult NOAA weather radio, or an official tide chart (available at insurance agencies, hardware stores, bookstores, and sometimes gas stations). The daily tides are also printed in the *Bar Harbor Times* newspaper, a local magazine called the *Acadia Weekly,* and an Acadia National Park publication, the *Beaver Log.*

Being able to identify the low- and high-tide lines on location is also an important skill. The low-tide line is often indicated by the presence of a long-bladed kelp. The high-tide line is marked by the uppermost occurrence of barnacles or black algae. To find the highest tide on the shore or beach, look for a black line, much like a bathtub ring, of dried rockweed. There are usually several lines, the highest being the spring tide, the wettest being the most recent high tide. This information is important to know whenever you decide to land. While I would never recommend leaving your kayak unattended or not tied to a tree, it is very helpful to know at what stage of the tide your boat will begin to float. I'll never forget the day I rounded an island to find a couple happily sleeping on the beach as their boat floated free fifty feet from shore. (I think they were "from away.")

Using the shoreline and intertidal zones as a ruler is an easy way not only to note the water level, but also, by looking again twenty minutes later, to determine whether the tide is ebbing (falling) or flooding (rising). After getting caught on a mudflat miles from your car, or having to paddle against a stiff current to get home at the end of a long day, you'll find that watching the tides quickly becomes second nature.

Freak tides and extreme tides are usually caused by planetary alignment and offshore storms. Several years ago, two friends of mine were on an overnight paddle in the Stonington area. There was a fifteen-foot tide during the night, and when they awoke, they were without boats. Fortunately, they had kept all their gear with them on shore, including their radio. They called for help, and an assisting vessel found their boats nearby. Know the tides, and always tie up your boat.

Tides also create currents as large volumes of water enter and leave bays and inlets. The resulting tidal currents range from barely detectable to strengths that even a very strong kayaker could not battle. When currents and wind oppose each other, large standing waves can be created.

Currents generally run the fastest where a channel is the deepest. In Bartlett Narrows this is particularly helpful to know. Bars or shoals also cause an increase in tidal current such as across the Moose Island Bar and at the entrance to Somes Sound. Currents can be used to your advantage, however; they form eddies behind islands, boats, and buoys and can be used to increase your speed if you're heading in the right direction.

The strength and direction of a current is most easily discerned by looking at a stationary object in the water, such as a moored boat, lobster buoy, or navigational marker. As these objects are pushed by the tide, their fixed end points in the direction from which the tide is coming. With a little experience, you can even estimate the current's strength. Notes on local currents and directions are given in the specific paddling trip descriptions that follow.

WIND AND WEATHER

> *I reverently believe that the maker who made us all*
> *makes everything in New England but the weather.*
> *I don't know who makes that, but I think it must be*
> *raw apprentices in the weather-clerk's factory...*
>
> —**MARK TWAIN**

The weather in Maine is, simply put, unpredictable. As the saying goes, "If you don't like the weather, wait a minute." It changes quickly and is variable from place to place. It can be foggy in Seal Harbor, raining in Bartlett Narrows, and sunny in Bar Harbor all at the same time.

Wind and weather are the dominant factors to be considered when planning a paddling trip. They determine whether you leave, where you go, and how long you stay out. An understanding of local weather patterns comes from reading the clouds and wind direction.

The prevailing winds during the summer (usually picking up in the afternoon) are southwest, because of a clockwise rotation of the high-pressure masses over the Atlantic. If the wind is from the southeast, it means that there is a counterclockwise rotation around a low pressure mass. The day will be gray, sometimes with fog and drizzle. Winds from the north or northwest usually follow southeast winds, bringing clear skies and great visibility; such winds are often strong. If the wind's from the northeast, get off the water—a storm is coming. Winds that blow at night often continue throughout the next day.

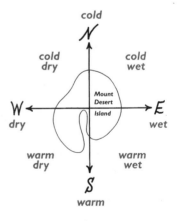

The wind directions and their general meaning is simple to understand when you remember this rhyme, first written in 1664: "When the wind is in the west, there it is the very best. But when the wind is in the east, 'tis neither good for man nor beast."

Understanding cloud shapes is one of the best ways to know what the weather is doing.

Cumulus clouds are heaped and look like puff-balls or cauliflower. Usually occurring in the late morning or early afternoon, they mean fair weather.

Cumulus

Stratus clouds are layered and sometimes wispy. "Mackerel scales and mares' tails make tall ships carry low sails," is a well-known saying describing stratus clouds that are "brushed out" by the always accompanying winds.

Stratus

Nimbus clouds are dark and gray; they carry rain and should serve as a warning for foul weather.

I'll never forget a day in Frenchman Bay when I learned about weather. I was paddling from Hadley Point to Bar Harbor in the afternoon, with a strong

Nimbus

northwest wind behind my back. I was offshore, across from the town of Hull's Cove, when over my shoulder I saw a tall, dark cumulonimbus storm cloud. I picked up the pace. My mind ran a mental check to find the location of my rain jacket. Murphy's Law said it was at the bottom of my dry bag. Murphy was right.

I looked behind me again and saw that the cloud was traveling faster than I. Two lightning bolts let free. This wasn't a storm I wanted to paddle through. I headed directly toward shore. The ensuing thunderclap reached me and stayed as a ringing in my ears. The skies soon opened and huge raindrops pummeled my head and shoulders. The storm was directly overhead as I reached the shore. I shivered in the cold and headed for shelter.

As quickly as the storm had come, it was gone. The cloud moved on. Along the trailing edge of the dark cloud, the sun streaks filtered down onto the black water. A full double rainbow framed the Porcupine Islands; at the end of the rainbow was Bar Harbor.

Here are a few more indicators that I have found useful in reading the weather. If there is a halo around the moon or sun, rain will usually come soon. The larger the halo, the closer the rain. This occurs because the light is reflecting off water droplets or ice crystals in the atmosphere.

Another popular saying—"Red sky at night, sailor's delight. Red sky in morning, sailor's take warning."—simplifies the phenomenon of a sunset seen through dry dusty air, which makes the colors stronger. Since our weather comes from the west, the sunset is the weather of tomorrow. Smoke is another weather indicator. Observe how the smoke rises from a fire or chimney. If it hangs low to the ground, the barometric pressure is dropping and poor weather or rain can be expected.

FOG

Besides lobster, the Maine coast is known for its fog. July and August, the two most popular months for paddling, are also two of the foggiest months of the year. Paddling in the fog can be a wonderful experience, however, for those with the proper skills. Fog helps to expand and widen your normal perspective of the coast, causing you to examine the micro instead of the macro, to take joy in the small and intimate details in front of you rather than the all-encompassing, sweeping views. Paddling in the fog also adds a mental challenge. Losing your sense of sight, you put full trust in your compass and navigational abilities. You feel the great amazement of heading into the dull whiteness for the first time, only to come upon an island right where the chart indicates it to be.

Fog is essentially a low-lying cloud. Two types of fog occur—and commonly I might add—in this area. Radiation fog is caused by the air cooling at night. This fog is light and thin and burns off by ten or eleven o'clock in the morning as the sun heats up the air. You can often see the sun shining above the fog bank. Advection fog does not burn off; it can linger for days or even weeks. This fog is thick and gray and is often accompanied by wind, making navigation difficult at best.

To paddle in the fog, you should be equipped with a foghorn on deck, a small flare gun, charts, and a handheld compass. A deck compass, though not needed, allows headings to be more easily and accurately followed. You should have good chart and compass skills and understand that, at least with current technology, kayaks are not clearly detectable by radar. Watch for other boats and let your presence be known. On foggy days it's best to paddle in areas that have little boat traffic.

SHARING LAND AND WATER

When paddling Maine waters, you share space, beauty, and resources with many others. There are certain laws (both written and otherwise) to which you should, out of respect and courtesy, adhere.

A local lobster boat and vacation home near Seal Harbor.
W. DAVID ANDREWS II.

ON THE WATER: Maine coastal communities depend on the ocean. Many residents are lobstermen, fishermen, or boat handlers. When you paddle, you are in the office of these men and women. Every time you and I get in the way, cause them to change course, or disturb them, they lose time and money—two commodities no mariner has to spare. Following some simple guidelines will allow paddlers and those working to coexist peacefully.

- Do not tie up or spend unnecessary time on boat ramps or loading floats. Others may be waiting.
- Although right-of-way rules dictate that power boats should yield to manually-propelled vessels such as sea kayaks, give way to other boats, for your craft is far more maneuverable.
- Do not paddle in heavily trafficked areas in the fog, and always use your foghorn.
- Never, ever, upon penalty of death, attempt to haul up, tamper with, or even sit near a lobster buoy. It is illegal to haul traps other than your own. Lobster pots are expensive, and lobstermen have little patience with those who interfere with their traps. Doing so is a serious cultural insult in coastal Maine.

ON THE LAND: Most Maine islands are privately owned. There is an ordinance from 1648 stating that the land between low and high tide is public for "fishing, fowling, and navigation," which used to be interpreted freely, and most anyone was welcome to land. In the spring of 1989 however, the Maine Supreme Court ruled in *Bell v. Town of Wells, Maine.* (also known as the Moody Beach case) that the law must be interperted exactly as it reads. Therefore, if you are stopping to fish, hunt, or navigate, you may do so, but if you are stopping to relieve yourself, eat lunch, or stretch your legs, you are technically trespassing.

Some owners do not mind if you land on their property; others do. As the number of sea kayakers has exploded along the Maine coast in the last few years, island visitation has increased dramatically and our welcome is wearing thin. Landing on a beach is a privilege, not a right. Your actions today will affect other sea kayakers in the future. The islands around Mount Desert Island are discussed in detail in the paddling trip descriptions, but here are some general guidelines regarding access.

Boaters may land if:

- Private landowners have posted that visitors are welcome.
- The land is owned by Acadia National Park, which forbids camping or fires but otherwise welcomes visitors (unless the land or island is protected because of bird activity).
- The land is owned by The Nature Conservancy, which welcomes visitors.
- A private island is under management of the Maine Island Trail Association, which welcomes members. Members should refer to their guidebook for island use guidelines.
- The land is publicly owned by the state or a town. Such land is open to all uses.

Landing on all other property is considered trespassing. Although "permissible trespassing" was common in the past, it is not now, and it will probably continue to decline as more and more people recreationally use the coast and islands. My general rule of thumb is that there are enough places to land where one is welcome or has been given permission; therefore, I try not to exacerbate the situation by landing on private property, particularly where there are "no trespassing" signs or nearby houses.

Remember, however, that if at any point you are in an emergency or if you need shelter from a storm, by the law of the sea, you may land where you choose.

I cannot stress individual responsibility enough. It is not only you who must pay the price for a misjudgment but also the individuals who risk their lives and safety to help you. Be honest about your abilities; don't take uncalculated risks.

O MOUNT DESERT ISLAND

Paddling Trips

Frenchman Bay

Frenchman Bay was originally called Douaguet, an Abenaki Indian word meaning "ground rising from the water." Alternative spellings include Adowake, Douakesc, Adowaukeag, and Waukeag. It is easy to understand the Abenaki word once you see Frenchman Bay for it is dotted with islands, many of which are tall and steep. They have been described as a "swarm of islands advancing out into the vast sparkling plane of the sea from the grim bastions of the coast like a cloud of skirmishers, the far-off islands emerging like monsters rising to take a breath. . . ."

The name Frenchman Bay originated from a conflict over control of this area between the French and English during the 1700s. French boats often prepared for battle in the bay before attacking English vessels. One story tells of an English captain who had to wait for days before he could enter the bay because of the many French ships. He wrote in his log about the "Frenchman's Bay." (Interestingly, farther up the coast, near Machias, close to the French-Canadian border, is Englishman Bay, perhaps with a similar history.)

The Mount Desert area was used extensively by Native Americans, particularly during the summer months. They would travel by river to spend the warmer months trading with each other, gathering food, and making tools. European settlement of the islands began in the mid- to late 1700s, at about the time of the American Revolution. Throughout the 1800s, as island and coastal populations grew, the bay was busy with traffic as boats carried lumber and granite down the coast to Boston and beyond.

A ferry service, beginning in 1870, brought wealthy summer visitors up from Boston and Rockland. Toward the end of the nineteenth century, Bar Harbor began to slowly change from a working harbor to a resort harbor for the yachts and schooners of the well-to-do. Today, Bar Harbor is an eclectic mix of lobster and fishing boats, power cruisers, sailboats, and ocean liners.

Frenchman Bay is a wonderful place to paddle. With many islands, an interesting social history, glacial geology, and ample wildlife, this bay offers a great variety of trips, from beginner to advanced, that can easily be modified to meet your needs. The following section contains descriptions for the Shore Route, The Porcupines, Ironbound Island, and Mount Desert Narrows. Enjoy.

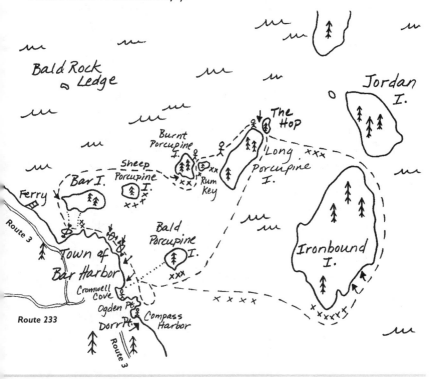

FRENCHMAN BAY

water access | x x x caution | landing site | point of interest | paddle trip

Shore Route

DIFFICULTY LEVEL
Beginner.

AVERAGE TRIP LENGTH
2–3 nautical miles.

PADDLE SUMMARY
In bad weather, or for the beginner paddler, I recommend the Shore Route. This trip can easily be shortened or expanded to suit your requirements. Intermediate paddlers (and on calm days, beginners as well) may want to add a loop to the Porcupine Islands.

While in the bay, you will be rewarded with views of Bar Harbor, the Shore Path, old rusticator mansions, and Compass Harbor, where a small hike can take you to the foundation of Old Farm, the former home of George Dorr, the Father of Acadia National Park. The beautiful mountains of Acadia National Park frame Bar Harbor's famous old homes. You can observe the islands', glacially carved profiles and glacial erratics. Bedrock known as the Bar Harbor formation makes up the shoreline. Frenchman Bay is also excellent for birding, with frequent sightings of bald eagles, cormorants, terns, gulls, and sometimes loons and eiders. Seals and porpoises commonly feed in the bay, and minke whales occasionally visit.

ITEMS OF INTEREST
HISTORY—A beautiful view of Bar Harbor with its historic rusticator mansions. A side hike takes you to the foundation of George Dorr's house.

GEOLOGY—Clear examples of glacial geology, including whalebacks and erratics. Views of the glacially sculpted mountains of Acadia National Park. Good examples of the bedrock Bar Harbor formation.

ECOLOGY—This area has excellent birding. Look for guillemots, bald eagles, great blue herons, cormorants and gulls.

CONDITIONS
The Shore Route is protected by the harbor breakwater. The only danger in foggy conditions is other boat traffic. This paddle is a good

choice when the weather prevents paddling elsewhere or when a short paddle is desired, such as in the evening or early morning.

ACCESS

BRIDGE ST.—Intersects with West St. Accessible at any tide; gentle beach and protected conditions. At low tide you can drive out on the Bar Harbor Bar. Park on West St.

TOWN RAMP—Although there is nearby parking, waves often make launching here somewhat difficult. Launching at the town beach, next to the ramp, is easier.

ALBERT MEADOW—Albert Meadow Rd. intersects with Main St. across from the town clock on the Village Green. There is ample parking, and the shore is only a short walk across a grassy lawn. The launch site is rocky but manageable.

LANDING SITES

CROMWELL COVE—Nice beach, accessible at all tides.

COMPASS HARBOR—Nice beach, accessible at all tides.

CAUTION AREAS

HARBOR BREAKWATER—This marks the end of protected water. There can be heavy boat traffic here.

THE PADDLE

From your put-in site, whether it be the Bar Harbor Bar, the town ramp, or Albert Meadow, head to the east corner of the downtown area, where you will soon come abeam of the Bar Harbor Motor Inn, a large gray building near the shore. Built in 1887, the structure was designed by architect William Ralph Emerson, who designed many mansions during this era. It originally housed the Reading Room, a club for wealthy rusticators to socialize and drink.

(See "Social History," p. 135.) The rusticators began coming to Bar Harbor in the 1870s to escape the hassle of city life and spend the summer enjoying the natural beauty of the area. Their lifestyle, however, was not rustic, but rather characterized by elaborate homes and busy social lives. The Reading Room is an excellent example of the social movement at the time. The guest book is impressive, including President William Taft in 1910. At its peak, 415 members gathered there to discuss poli-

tics, government, and the latest town gossip. By 1922, as Prohibition came into effect, only ten members remained.

(See "Geology," p. 95.) Along the shoreline just below the inn, you will find examples of the Bar Harbor formation bedrock. From the sharply defined layers, you can tell that this rock is sedimentary; it was laid as the floor of an ancient ocean 380 million years ago. Note the dark red and brown hues and the upward tilt of the layers toward the south. This rock, very common in Frenchman Bay on the southern side of the Porcupine Islands, forms a weak shoreline that erodes easily, leaving unusual shapes such as chimneys, keyholes, and caves.

Heading southward, you will see a grassy lawn. This public park, called Albert Meadow, marks the beginning of the Shore Path. Established more than a hundred years ago, it is the oldest "formal" hiking trail on the island (several Indian trails are older). The Fire of '47, which burned a large number of mansions and caused more than two million dollars in property damage, did not burn this area; as you can see, several of the old mansions remain. West Street escaped as well, leaving many of the rusticator mansions on the water's edge standing.

The first large house you will see is the Balance Rock Inn, built in 1901. Gray with yellow trim, this bed-and-breakfast sits behind a beautiful hedge of wild roses. In front of this house is Balance Rock, a classic example of a glacial erratic. This boulder of Lucerne granite was carried by glaciers from its point of origin, nineteen miles to the north.

After a series of smaller modern houses, you'll come to a small white gateway leading to the Breakwater Inn. This bed-and-breakfast, built in 1904 as a summer cottage, was renovated in 1991 and placed on the National Register of Historic Places on March 26, 1992. The brown and yellow inn marks the end of the Shore Path.

The current Redwood house.
W. DAVID ANDREWS II.

The light green house with dark green trim is called Byde-a-while. It was built in 1896. Redwood, the next house, was built in 1879 by W. R. Emerson, the architect of the Reading Room. Redwood, one of the earliest shingle-style houses, was placed on the National Register of Historic Places in 1978. The name came from two red maples on the property at the time.

The final rusticator cottage, sitting on a beautiful point of land directly across from the harbor breakwater, is the Kenarden Lodge. It replaced the original Kenarden, which was built in 1892 for John S. Kennedy and was one of the largest cottages at the time—it even had its own power plant. The first house was torn down in the 1960s. The present mansion is owned by the grandson of the founder of the Campbell Soup Company.

The original Kenarden house about 1900. Note the people on the lawn.
BAR HARBOR HISTORICAL SOCIETY.

Use caution when paddling between the Kenarden Lodge and the harbor breakwater. I recommend staying close to the shoreline, as working and pleasure boats use this channel heavily. I've often had to

The current Kenarden house.
W. DAVID ANDREWS II.

use my foghorn here and sometimes even wait my turn to pass through. This also marks the end of the protected water of Bar Harbor; conditions are often rougher past this point.

After the Kenarden Lodge, you will pass Cromwell Cove and Ogden Point before arriving at Compass Harbor. The land surrounding Compass Harbor is a small part of Acadia National Park and has a series of hiking trails within the woods. This pretty cove is a wonderful place to land and take a short hike to explore. Be sure to pull your boat above the high-water mark lest it float away without you. Climb the embankment on the southern half of the cove and you will find the trails.

The square foundation in the water near Dorr Point (the southernmost point of the cove) is the remains of a saltwater swimming pool. These pools were common in the rusticator era and still are today. The pool belonged to George Dorr, the single most significant man in the formation of what would eventually become Acadia National Park. Dorr was known to swim in this pool daily in both summer and winter!

A particularly rewarding adventure is to follow the trail southward from Dorr Point to the foundation of Old Farm, George Dorr's house, which was originally built in 1876 by Charles Dorr, his father. Follow the long set of granite steps up the hill and you will come upon the brick and granite foundation of a covered terrace in the front of the house. You can make out several rooms, terraces, cellar windows, and wells as the foundation continues back into the woods away from the water. Look for the group of cedars that marked the circular driveway and

Old Farm, home of George Dorr, Father of Acadia.
BAR HARBOR HISTORICAL SOCIETY.

other large trees that once flanked the house. (Several pieces of art and dishes from the house remain in the Bar Harbor Historical Society along with photographs of the interior.) Please remember to leave all as you found it, including bricks.

George Dorr lived in this house near the sea, devoting his life to exploring and learning about Mount Desert Island. In 1940, at the age of eighty-six, Dorr moved to Storm Beach, the caretaker's cottage, which stands today on Old Farm Road and is still used by the park. Soon afterward, he transferred ownership of Old Farm to Acadia National Park. Dorr died in 1944. In 1946, the Park surveyed the house, then badly in need of repair, and recommended that it be destroyed. Old Farm was eventually demolished in 1951.

The demolition of this irreplaceable piece of history was a great misfortune, for now all that remains is a bare foundation that few hikers know about and even fewer ever find. We can learn only from its overgrown brick floors and broken granite stairs.

To complete the Shore Route paddle, return to your boat and follow the shoreline back. Intermediate paddlers may choose to further explore the Porcupine Islands, as described on the following pages.

The Porcupines

DIFFICULTY LEVEL
Intermediate.

AVERAGE TRIP LENGTH
4–6 nautical miles.

PADDLE SUMMARY
The Porcupines trip is an easily accessible paddle that can be shortened or expanded to meet your needs. In bad weather, or for the beginner paddler, I recommend the Shore Route as an abridged version of this trip. The Shore Route and The Porcupines can be combined for a full-day trip. *(See the Frenchman Bay map on p. 29.)*

While in the bay, you will be rewarded with views of Bar Harbor, the Shore Path, old rusticator mansions, and the greater Frenchman Bay area. The beautiful mountains of Acadia National Park act as a backdrop.

You will have the opportunity to observe the islands' glacially shaped profile. They are good examples of *roches moutonnées,* commonly referred to as whalebacks. You can also see several glacial erratics, the bedrock known as the Bar Harbor formation, a magnificent intrusion of gabbro-diorite, cobblestone beaches, and cliffs.

Frenchman Bay is excellent for birding, with sightings of bald eagles, great blue herons, and cliff-dwelling guillemots, along with cormorants, terns, gulls, and sometimes loons and eiders. Seals and porpoises commonly feed in the bay; occasionally minke whales pay a visit in August.

ITEMS OF INTEREST

HISTORY—Views of Bar Harbor and its historic rusticator mansions.

GEOLOGY—Clear examples of glacial geology, including whalebacks and erratics, as well as the glacially sculpted mountains of Acadia National Park. A keyhole, sandbars and cobble beaches can be seen, as well as examples of the bedrock Bar Harbor formation and igneous gabbro-diorite.

ECOLOGY—Excellent birding includes guillemots, bald eagles, great blue herons, cormorants, and gulls. Seals, porpoises, and occasionally minke whales are also present.

CONDITIONS

The highly variable weather is a predominant factor in the intermediate difficulty rating of this trip. Although usually calm in the morning and evening, this area is prone to strong winds that commonly begin about noon. Light to moderate winds (0–15 knots) are ideal for paddling this route. Even in areas protected by the breakwater, Frenchman Bay can develop large seas, particularly if the wind is from a northerly direction. Fog is also common and can engulf the bay quickly. Because of heavy boat traffic, the bay is very dangerous in these conditions and should be avoided.

ACCESS

Same as Shore Route access, p. 31.

ISLAND OWNERSHIP

BAR ISLAND—Part Acadia National Park, part private.

SHEEP PORCUPINE—Acadia National Park.

BURNT PORCUPINE—Private.

RUM KEY—Private.

LONG PORCUPINE—The Nature Conservancy.

THE HOP—Acadia National Park.

BALD PORCUPINE—Acadia National Park.

LANDING SITES

RUM KEY, NORTH SIDE—A good beach for landing except in strong north winds.

LONG PORCUPINE, MIDPOINT NORTH SIDE—Exposed only at mid-tide. Easy landing site surrounded by big, flat rocks.

THE HOP—Sandbar between Long Porcupine and The Hop exposed at low tides. The Hop also accessible at high tide on the north shore.

COMPASS HARBOR—Nice beach, accessible at all tides.

CROMWELL COVE—Nice beach, accessible at all tides.

DO NOT LAND: Long Porcupine, mid-island south side—The waves are usually too rough here.

DO NOT LAND: Sheep Porcupine—Bald eagle territory. Your landing would be extremely detrimental. *(See "Environmental Kayaking," page 146.)*

CAUTION AREAS

BAR HARBOR BAR, EAST SIDE—Extensive mudflat exposed for two hours before and after low tide. You cannot land here but instead must paddle around Bar Island to reach Bridge St. or land at the town beach.

SHEEP PORCUPINE, SOUTHEAST—A submerged rock creates breaking waves during mid- to high tide. Stay well offshore.

BURNT PORCUPINE, SOUTHEAST—Large swells and rough surf occur in strong southerly winds.

BURNT PORCUPINE / RUM KEY CROSSING—Large swells can develop in this narrow passage.

RUM KEY / LONG PORCUPINE CROSSING—Large swells can develop in this passage.

BALD PORCUPINE, SOUTH—Rebounding waves can occur on this exposed side, creating a large chop. Stay well offshore.

THE PADDLE

I have heard of an Abenaki legend that tells of a great chief on the top of Cadillac Mountain. Frustrated by a continual disturbance during an important tribal meeting, he picked up several porcupines and threw them into the bay. There they landed and remain today: the Porcupine Islands. The current names of the islands—Bar Island, Sheep Porcupine, Burnt Porcupine, Long Porcupine, and Bald Porcupine—changed many times before the turn of this century, which often confuses the examination of old charts, books, and histories. Nonetheless, these islands have always been, and will always remain, a "family" of porcupines. For a while in 1910, both Bar Harbor and Gouldsboro claimed jurisdiction over Bar Island, but the islands remained together when Gouldsboro eventually gained the rights to all the Porcupines.

This trip begins at Bar Island, which was bought by David Rodick during Bar Harbor's heyday at the turn of the twentieth century. He was also the owner of the 400-room Rodick House in Bar Harbor, the largest hotel in Maine. Around 1945, Bar Island was sold to the Rockefellers, who, in turn, gave the island to Acadia National Park. Today, the island still belongs to the park except for one small privately owned parcel with a year-round resident. There were two failed attempts (in 1909 and 1960) to build a bridge to Bar Island to make it accessible during all tides.

The Bar Harbor Bar is one of the best places to watch birds on Mount Desert Island. They are best observed feeding during low tide. Also take a moment to examine the sandbar created by tidal currents and glacial sand.

(See "Social History," p. 135.) Looking to the west from the bar into the large cove, you can see mansions that were unharmed during the Fire of '47. The high dock extending out into the water is in front of the College of the Atlantic library. (This small, nontraditional, accredited college offers both undergraduate and graduate degrees in human ecology.) The beautiful stone mansion to the left of the library houses several classrooms, administrative offices, and a natural history museum; the museum is open to the public and is highly recommended. This mansion, named The Turrets, is another reminder of the rusticator days. To the right of the College of the Atlantic is the terminal of the *Bluenose* Ferry, which offers service to Yarmouth, Nova Scotia.

Low tide exposes an expanse of mudflat to the east of the Bar

Harbor bar, so you will not be able to paddle here during that time. Trust me, it is a long walk through knee-deep mud, so plan your departure and return accordingly. (It took me days to get the mud out from under my toenails.)

(See "Geology," p. 95.) If you continue paddling around the north side of Bar Island, you'll see on the most northwest corner a striking example of a glacial erratic perched on the edge of a rock just above the high-tide line. I've often seen great blue herons here. Keep a sharp watch; the birds blend in with the shoreline very well.

(See "Social History," p. 135.) As you approach the eastern end of Bar Island, take a moment to look at Bar Harbor and imagine the great rusticator days. The town was once filled with huge mansions, similar to the few still remaining on West Street and the Shore Path. The harbor was dotted with great sailing ships, and the center of town contained huge and lavish hotels. The mountains in the background would someday become part of Acadia National Park. They are, in order from right to left, Cadillac Mountain, Dorr Mountain, Huguenot Head, and Champlain Mountain.

Continuing eastward, you'll come upon Sheep Porcupine, which was occupied throughout the 1860s and '70s; it had four structures, including a store on the northeast corner. During the 1880s, sheep grazed here. As you round the island, watch for a submerged rock on the south side; it creates an unexpected breaking wave during mid- to high tide. On the east side of Sheep Porcupine Island is Green Bell #7, which you may find useful for getting yourself oriented in fog.

(See "Environmental Kayaking," p. 146.) Sheep Porcupine has a bald eagle nest, reportedly eight feet in diameter and weighing more than a ton, but it is extremely difficult to see. Do not land on this island. Kayak-

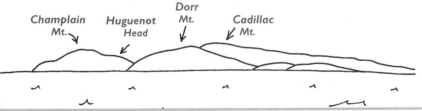

The mountains of Acadia as seen from the Porcupine Islands.

ers and other boaters should stay at least one-fourth mile (one-half the distance across the channel) from the island to help reduce the human harassment of this pair of eagles. During nesting season, March through August, you might want to pass only on the north side of the island to further reduce impact. Eagles are very susceptible to disturbance, and this pair in particular is subject to heavy boat traffic.

Between Sheep Porcupine and Burnt Porcupine Islands is the main channel connecting upper and lower Frenchman Bay. This deep channel is used by large vessels traveling within the bay; use caution when crossing, especially in fog. The wind and waves also can be strong in this area.

(See "Marine Ecology," p. 109, and "Environmental Kayaking," p. 146.) Nevertheless, it is worth spending time in this channel, though preferably near an island for shelter and safety. Watch the water's surface for gray heads and dark fins. My own personal theory is that the water funnels through this channel, and eddies are created behind Sheep and Burnt Islands. The eddies harbor pockets of fish, which attract seals, porpoises, and whales. You will see a crescent-shaped black fin or possibly a small breaching body when porpoises swim by or feed. They usually travel in pairs or groups. Harbor seals will often follow your kayak. Minke whales, needless to say, are hard to miss.

(See "Geology," p. 95.) Burnt Porcupine was the site of several small fishing camps during the 1880s. The north side of the island has a gently sloping shoreline, the perfect example of a glacial feature called a *roche moutonnée*. The French term means "sheep rock"—a logical choice given its shape. If you prefer an easier word, call it a whaleback. Looking at any of the Porcupine Islands, you will see this general shape: gently sloping on the north side, steep cliffs on the south side. Although the various rock types helped determine this asymmetry, it was mostly caused by the pressure and plucking effect of the ice sheet as it moved southward.

(See "Geology," p 95.) On the westward side of Burnt Porcupine, the bedrock Bar Harbor formation becomes visible, showing a broad horizontal layer of whitish rock. This vein leads to a geologic wonder called the Keyhole, a tall cleft that leads inward toward the center of the island. This chasm, which ends at a small cobble beach, was caused

The shoreline of Burnt Porcupine shows the layered Bar Harbor formation. The white stripes lead toward the Keyhole.
W. DAVID ANDREWS II.

by water and ice eroding and widening a crack within the Bar Harbor formation.

It is possible to paddle into the Keyhole under the proper conditions (it is about two to three feet wide), but caution should be used. I was out with a group of friends one evening when Chris, a fellow guide, decided to enter. The waves amplified through this narrow passage. He tried to brace, hit the rock wall, and snapped his new wooden paddle in half. Although you might be able to surf a wave in, there is little turning room once inside, and it is impossible to paddle on the way out. I would recommend attempting to enter only when the sea is completely flat.

The opening to the Keyhole.
W. DAVID ANDREWS II.

The south side of Burnt Porcupine. Note the differences in rock composition and coloration.
W. DAVID ANDREWS II

On the south side of Burnt Porcupine is one of my favorite shorelines. Overlying the Bar Harbor formation is a whitish rock with intrusions of gabbro-diorite. The result is a small-grained, dark gray band vertically oriented within a jagged, rough white rock. It is an unusual and complex pattern. Remember to use caution in this area because of the rebounding waves. On the southeast side you can clearly see the layered Bar Harbor formation, like that seen earlier on the other Porcupines.

(See "Environmental Kayaking," p. 146.) Rum Key sits on the east side of Burnt Porcupine. Large swells sometimes form in the passage between these two islands, so use caution. I remember heading out one summer day in light winds. After taking a break on Rum Key, I tried to paddle toward the south side of Burnt into a very strong southwest wind that had arisen during my break. After heading into four-foot swells for several minutes and making no headway, I was forced to retreat and travel on the lee side to get back home.

Rum Key is a small, heavily used island, and justifiably so, because it is a great place to take a break. This island needs extra care—please tread lightly. On the beach you will find a generous quantity of red, porous, egg-shaped stones. Though they may appear to be igneous or metamorphic rock, they are, in fact, pieces of brick that have been ground smooth by the sea, similar to sea glass. Bricks are commonly used as weights in lobster traps, so it is not unusual to find these "sea bricks" along the Maine coast. Remember to leave them, however, for others to enjoy.

In the summer of 1995, hurricane Felix sent ten- to fifteen-foot swells up the coast of Mount Desert Island. I visited Rum Key just before the waves arrived and again four days later. When I returned, I found a different beach from the one I had been using for years. In a mere four days, the waves had moved several tons of cobblestones (roughly the size of baseballs) from the north side to the northeastern side of the island, exposing some rock ledges and burying others. The force of the ocean and waves never ceases to amaze and impress me.

You may prefer to head back at this point, or continue on to Long Porcupine and the Hop. If you proceed, watch for large swells that can form between Rum Key and Long Porcupine—use caution.

Long Porcupine is a wonderfully beautiful, dramatic, and historic island. Along with its small tagalong, The Hop, this island was used for haying, grazing, logging, and fishing. At times there were seasonal fishing camps here. Long Porcupine was still used for economic profit well into this century; 4,000 cords of pulpwood were removed in 1938 and sent to a mill in Bucksport. The island became the property of The Nature Conservancy in 1977.

(See "Marine Ecology," p. 109.) The interior of the island is home to osprey, eagles, and a small herd of deer. From the shore, Long Porcupine offers wonders on all sides. On the west side, the 165-foot cliffs are home to many black guillemots. Cousins to the Atlantic puffin, the tub-shaped guillemots, with their triangular eggs, are my favorite bird.

On the south side of the island is a cobble beach, but the water is usually far too rough to land here. On the north side, however, is a

Cliffs on the western shore of Long Porcupine.
W. DAVID ANDREWS II

beach exposed at three-quarters and lower tides that is a safe and pleasant stopping place.

(See "Environmental Kayaking," p. 146.) The Hop, east of Long Porcupine, is connected at low tide by a small sandbar, called a tombolo. The Hop was the fishing center for the bay during the late 1800s, when the protected waters were dotted with herring weirs and wooden skiffs, and the air was filled with the clanking and banging of activity. This island was recently bought by Acadia National Park. Given its limited size, the Hop needs special care—please tread lightly. The Hop and Long Island are also bald eagle territory; please do not hike into the interior of the islands or spend prolonged periods of time there, particularly around the tombolo.

The crossing to Bald Porcupine is quite open, so be sure to use caution. Bald Porcupine, which is connected to the Bar Harbor breakwater, is currently owned by the park. Like many of the islands settled in the eighteenth and nineteenth centuries, Bald was cleared and used for hay and sheep. It is reported that around 1870 a small village called Pogyville existed on Bald Porcupine (pogies are schooling fish harvested for their oil and as bait), although this seems unlikely, given the geology of the island. Bald's inhibiting steep cliffs make it next to impossible to reach the island's summit. The only beach faces seaward, and it is a rare day when a boat can land there. Given the many name changes that have occurred over the years, it's very possible that Pogeyville actually was on another of the Porcupines.

Beware of the chop that can form on the south side of the island from reflecting waves even on relatively calm days. I thought I had an iron stomach until I experienced the chop that can occur here. This is not a good place to get into trouble. The island is also eagle territory; stay several hundred yards offshore.

Looking southward from Bald Porcupine, you can see Egg Rock Light. Built in 1875, when ferry service began in Frenchman Bay, Egg Rock, like other Maine lighthouses, has a history of hazards and hardships. Five months after its construction, gale-driven waves moved its giant bell thirty feet and washed away the fuel shed. In 1887, a similar storm severely damaged the property, followed in 1900 by a storm that washed away the boathouse. A fog-signal horn was added to the lighthouse in 1904, and in 1907 it operated for 1,813 hours, a total of 75 full days of fog!

In 1976, the lighthouse and foghorn were automated, and after 101 years of service, the small rock outcrop was no longer inhabited by humans. In all those years, only one keeper died while in service; he drowned while rowing ashore to Bar Harbor. Egg Rock is one of the few square lighthouses on the Maine coast; most lights are cylindrical to disperse the force of wind and waves.

From Bald Porcupine, I would recommend following the Shore Route back to Bar Harbor.

Ironbound Island

DIFFICULTY LEVEL

Advanced, due to open crossings, remoteness, and exposure. This trip should be attempted only by experienced kayakers.

AVERAGE TRIP LENGTH

8–10 nautical miles.

PADDLE SUMMARY

The circumnavigation of Ironbound Island, starting from Bar Harbor, is an advanced, all-day excursion that is demanding and breathtaking. Stops along the Porcupines can be incorporated on the way. One of the first island settlements, Ironbound has an unusual history due to its rich soil. The tall, dramatic cliffs of the island are broken only by keyholes, caves, and long cobble beaches. *(See the Frenchman Bay chart on p. 29.)*

ITEMS OF INTEREST

HISTORY—Ironbound Island is one of the first islands in this area to be settled, and it had one of the longest-running island schools.

GEOLOGY—Igneous rock, including gabbro-diorite and Bar Harbor formation. Keyholes, caves, arches, and pillars lace the island. Cliffs of 100-plus feet.

ECOLOGY—Old-growth forest exists on Ironbound. Many birds and marine mammals feed in the area.

CONDITIONS

This full-day paddle should be attempted only on an unusually calm day of light winds (0–10 knots). The middle of Frenchman Bay and the southern tip of Ironbound are open and exposed. You are likely to face a headwind during the homeward paddle due to prevailing southwest winds. Winds from the north are usually too strong to permit this trip. Weather in this area is highly variable, and afternoon winds can be strong. Fog can also engulf the bay quickly.

ACCESS

Same as Shore Route access, p. 31.

LANDING SITES

Refer to The Porcupines trip for stops within that area.

DO NOT LAND: Ironbound Island—Private property. The owners have requested that boats not land anywhere on the island except in an emergency.

CAUTION AREAS

FRENCHMAN BAY—This crossing is long and exposed in any wind. It should be attempted only in good weather and light winds. Watch out for boat traffic.

IRONBOUND ISLAND, SOUTH END—This entire side is completely open and exposed to the full force of the sea. Large swells break against the cliffs, causing reflected waves. Stay well offshore.

THE PADDLE

Before beginning this trip, read the preceding trip description for The Porcupines. It discusses Frenchman Bay out to The Hop and contains information needed for the trip to and from Ironbound.

Ironbound is a dramatic and wild island with a long and interesting human history. As seen from Bar Harbor, its gently sloping west side gives little indication of the 100- to 120-foot cliffs dropping straight into the sea on the east side. I recommend circumnavigating in a counter-clockwise direction if the wind is from the southwest. This will allow the exposed leg of the trip, the western shore, to be paddled in the morning and the return trip, often into a headwind, to be among the Porcupine Islands.

You may choose to head straight for the southern tip of Ironbound if there is no wind, or paddle to Long Porcupine before crossing over to the western shore of Ironbound. This shoreline, although gradual in elevation, is rough and exposed to the full force of the open ocean.

The first settler arrived on Ironbound in 1790, almost 100 years earlier than on the other islands in Frenchman Bay. (Only Bartlett Island in Blue Hill Bay was settled earlier, in 1767.) At the time, there were fewer than forty families on Mount Desert Island. By 1815, there were as many as eight families on Ironbound, and in 1817, a school opened on the island. It ran for eight to ten weeks a year and was headed by an island resident. It operated for forty-two years, longer than most island schools, before finally closing its doors in 1859.

(See "Social History," p. 135.) This year-round, self-sufficient community was unlike any others in Frenchman Bay in that it had sufficient soil to support year-round farming and cattle raising. Limited pogy pressing, shipbuilding, logging, and silver mining also occurred. By the turn of the century, however, many residents had moved to the mainland, and the island was inhabited only during the summer months. In 1944, several fires of unknown origin burned many of the old homes. Today the island is occupied during the summer by a local family who have owned property on Ironbound Island for more than a hundred years.

As you approach the southern tip, be aware of the raw exposure here. Looking southward, you can see Egg Rock Light. (This light is described in more detail in the write-up of Bald Porcupine—page 44.)

(See "Geology," p. 95.) Nestled on the south side of Ironbound are several sea arches, small caves, and pillars created by the extreme force of the sea against the soft bedrock. With careful observation, you should be able to find quite a few. The tall cliffs are made of the bedrock Bar Harbor formation, though they are more gray in color than the examples of brown-hued Bar Harbor formation found in other parts of the bay. On the east side of the island you will be able to clearly see the rock layers. There are also many dikes of gabbro-diorite.

At the southeastern tip of the island is a deep sea cave, similar to the famous Thunder Hole located in Acadia National Park. Although crashing waves do not create as loud a noise here as in Thunder Hole, this cave does extend back and upward, ending in a bed of perfectly rounded cobblestones. It would be very unsafe to attempt entering this cave, due to the exposure and large swells that break here.

Just north of the cave is a keyhole, called the Devil's Den, similar to the one on Burnt Porcupine. This keyhole is the result of water and ice plucking away at a crack in the bedrock. The Devil's Den is approximately ten feet wide and extends twenty to thirty feet back. Entry is recommended only on the calmest of days.

As you paddle this eastern shore, notice the island vegetation. The forest on Ironbound is different from that on the other bay islands. The trees are older and the undergrowth is more dense. There are reportedly several old-growth stands on the island, although as recently as 1938 pulpwood was removed from the northeast corner.

Within a mile, you will turn toward the west and pass through Halibut Hole, between Ironbound and Jordan Islands. Tidal currents can be very strong. On an incoming tide, they run from east to west; on an outgoing tide, they run from west to east. Note the gentle upward rise of the northern shore compared to the steep southern shore—a profile typical of Frenchman Bay islands.

From here, cross toward Long Porcupine or The Hop and use these islands as protection as you head westward back to Bar Harbor.

Mount Desert Narrows

DIFFICULTY LEVEL
Beginner.

AVERAGE TRIP LENGTH
Up to 10 nautical miles.

PADDLE SUMMARY
Mount Desert Narrows is a beautiful beginner paddle and a wonderful location for a sunset trip. The area offers some unusual geology and several interesting places to visit—including the Thompson Island Bridge, a salt marsh, and a mudflat. The trip may begin at either the Thompson Island picnic area or Hadley Point. A full-day option is available, leaving from Thompson Island and including The Ovens.

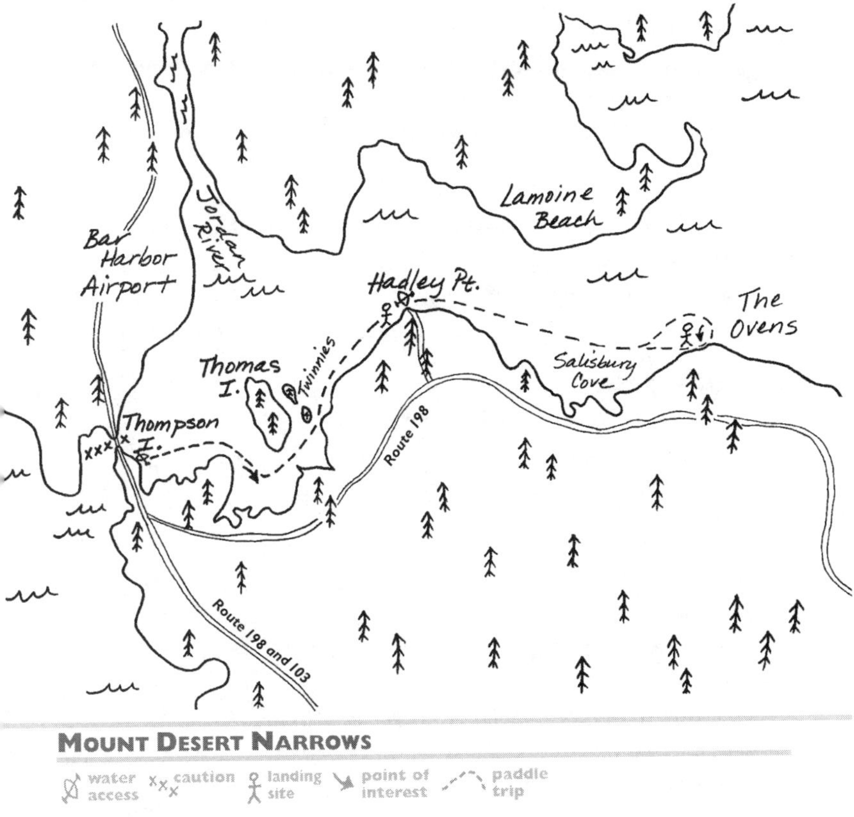
Jordan River
Lamoine Beach
Bar Harbor Airport
Hadley Pt.
The Ovens
Thomas I.
Twinnies
Salisbury Cove
Thompson I.
Route 198
Route 198 and 103
MOUNT DESERT NARROWS
water access
caution
landing site
point of interest
paddle trip

ITEMS OF INTEREST

HISTORY—The Thompson Island bridge and a shell midden are in this area.

GEOLOGY—Bedrock, including shorelines of Ellsworth schist and Bar Harbor formation, and The Ovens, a group of sea caves.

ECOLOGY—Salt marshes and mudflats attract many birds, including great blue herons and eagles.

CONDITIONS

This trip is another option in moderate to strong winds (10 knots or higher) and fog. Any wind direction is acceptable, although watch due-west winds, as they are usually quite strong.

If you begin your trip at the Thompson Island picnic area, it is very important to watch the water level. This area is a large mudflat for two hours on either side of low tide. If you begin at Hadley Point, do not drive onto the sand. It is very soft and is known to swallow cars. (Once the water was lapping at my tires before I was pulled out!)

ACCESS

THOMPSON ISLAND PICNIC AREA—Thompson Island, on Rte. 3 across from the Visitor Center. Ample parking.

HADLEY POINT—Hadley Point Rd. intersects Rte. 3 at the top of the hill between Northeast Creek and Salisbury Cove. Ample parking.

ISLAND OWNERSHIP

THOMPSON—Acadia National Park.

THOMAS—Private.

THE TWINNIES—Private.

LANDING SITES

HADLEY POINT—Sometimes crowded but a nice beach and picnic area.

THE OVENS—Cobble beach. Respect private property by not climbing the staircase.

DO NOT STOP: Within Thomas Bay, on Thomas Island, or on The Twinnies. These islands are fragile, and the wildlife is vulnerable to human intrusion.

CAUTION AREAS

THOMPSON ISLAND AREA—Exposed mudflat for two hours on either side of low tide. The current under the bridge runs west to east on an incoming tide and east to west on an outgoing tide.

HADLEY POINT—Do not drive on the sand.

THE PADDLE

This paddle begins at the Thompson Island put-in site and follows the Mount Desert Island shoreline to The Ovens. Note, however, that during low tide, you must put in at Hadley Point.

Thompson Island was originally called Bark Island in 1785 because of the tree bark that was collected and used in the tanning of skins and hides. In 1792, Cornelius Thompson, a commander in the American Revolution, was given the island by the heirs of Sieur Antoine de la Mothe Cadillac. This was early in the history of island settlement and ownership; at that time, only Bartlett and Ironbound Islands were settled, and there were only a few dozen families on Mount Desert Island.

(See "Social History," p. 135.) Thompson Island was, and still is, very important due to its proximity to Mount Desert Island and the mainland. The formation of the Mount Desert Island Bridge Corporation in 1836 was a turning point in the history of Thompson Island, which then became the most traveled and visited island along the Maine coast. The bridge greatly increased the accessibility of Mount Desert Island, and in fact enabled Thomas Cole to come here in 1842. This famous painter, and others, would forever change the course of Bar Harbor's history.

The Thompson family ran and maintained the bridge and collected the tolls until the 1920s, when the bridge became the property of the state. After the Thompson family moved, Thompson Island housed several dance halls and even a roller skating rink. In 1944, the island came under the ownership of Acadia National Park. Several of the old foundations can be seen today behind the visitor center built by the park in 1984.

(See "Geology," p. 95.) As you paddle east from Thompson Island toward Thomas Bay, you can see the shoreline made of Ellsworth schist. Schist, a metamorphic rock, was originally deposited in layers, later to be heated and pressurized. Now it is twisted and complex, resembling marble cake. The schist along this shoreline is layered volcanic ash, in contrast to the rest of the island schist, which is layered clay and sand from an ancient ocean that existed 450 million years ago.

Within one mile, you will enter Thomas Bay, sheltered by Thomas Island and The Twinnies. A salt marsh—one of the richest and most productive ecosystems known—exists where Northeast Creek enters the bay.

This cove, a good place to examine closely the rich ecology of salt marshes and mudflats, is home to many organisms and birds, including bald eagles, osprey, great blue herons, and smaller seabirds. You can't miss the beautiful view of several mountains that are part of Acadia National Park. Please do not land in Thomas Bay or on any of the islands.

THE SEA KAYAKER'S GUIDE

The ecology here is fragile, and the wildlife is extremely vulnerable to human disturbance.

(See "Social History," p. 135.) Thomas Island has two freshwater springs and evidence of a shell midden, a Native American garbage site. Over time, the decaying shells neutralize the surrounding soil, thereby preserving materials such as bone, food, and tools. It is from these sites that Maine archaeologists learn about the history of Abenaki Indians and the ecology and environment of their time. Neither Thomas Island nor The Twinnies (named for these two islands' identical appearance) has any evidence of European settlement. Thomas Island has been logged many times (there once was a very active lumber mill on Northeast Creek) and has also been used for pasturage.

Leaving Thomas Bay, you'll see Hadley Point a mile to the east, the only put-in site for this trip during low tide. It is a nice landing place and often popular with picnicking families.

Salisbury Cove, one mile east of Hadley Point, is another beautiful inlet that should be explored. The Mount Desert Island Biological Laboratory is located here in the far southeast corner, though it is difficult to see from the water. Originally founded in Harpswell, Maine, the lab moved to the island in 1921. The facility's relocation and subsequent success are one example of the artistic and intellectual trend that followed the arrival of Thomas Cole and the rusticators in the mid-nineteenth century. The laboratory is only open to the public during the summer. Tours are available and highly recommended.

(See "Geology," p. 95.) Another mile to the east are The Ovens, one of two substantial cave sites on Mount Desert Island (the other is Anemone Cave). Nestled within the loose sedimentary layers of Bar Harbor formation, these wave- and ice-plucked caves are accessible only by boat. A kayaker's dream! Some are as large as twenty-five feet wide, fifteen feet high, and ten to twenty feet deep. At low tide, you can walk into the caves; at high tide you can paddle into them. There is also an opening, or eyehole, you can walk through; it's called Cathedral Rock.

The Ovens have long been a favorite place to visit. An 1887 guide to Mount Desert Island tells of the wondrous caves and recommends them highly. In the summer of 1994, a large section of cliff face fell,

The Ovens at low tide. Note Cathedral Rock,
the opening on the far left.

creating a debris pile at the water's edge. It was fascinating to arrive one day and see such a difference; it gave me a much better appreciation and understanding of geologic change.

After visiting The Ovens, you may choose to continue along this shoreline, or you can return toward Hadley Point or Thompson Island either via the Mount Desert Island shoreline or the Trenton shoreline across the Narrows.

Blue Hill Bay

Nestled between the Brooklin peninsula and Mount Desert Island, Blue Hill Bay extends out from the mouth of the Union River, which flows down from Ellsworth. Its welcoming and protected waters, filled with islands both small and large, have a long and rich history. The area was avoided by early explorers because of the long conflict between the French and English, resulting in the French and Indian War (1755–63), which prevented safe exploration. In fact, on a 1691 chart, Blue Hill Bay is completely omitted, whereas nearby Penobscot Bay is described in detail.

Reliable charting of the area came only after the war, and European settlement followed soon afterward. By 1760, Tinker and Hog Islands were settled, and in the 1770s there was a homestead on Alley Island and a mill on Long Island. Most of the islands in Blue Hill Bay were settled and occupied throughout the 1800s.

In 1837, in true Yankee fashion, several of the islands in Blue Hill Bay applied for their own township, separate from that of Mount Desert Island. The original name of the township, Seville, was quickly changed to Seaville due to a misspelling. Bartlett, Hardwood, and Tinker were the primary islands, hosting town meetings and housing three schools with sixty-five students combined. In 1858, when Seaville disassembled, Bartlett Island became the property of Mount Desert, while the other islands became affiliated with the mainland town of Tremont.

With its varied wildlife, beautiful granite shores, and many islands of early and current occupation, Blue Hill Bay is one of my favorite areas for boating. The following section contains paddling trips for Bartlett Narrows, the circumnavigation of Bartlett Island, and Seal Cove.

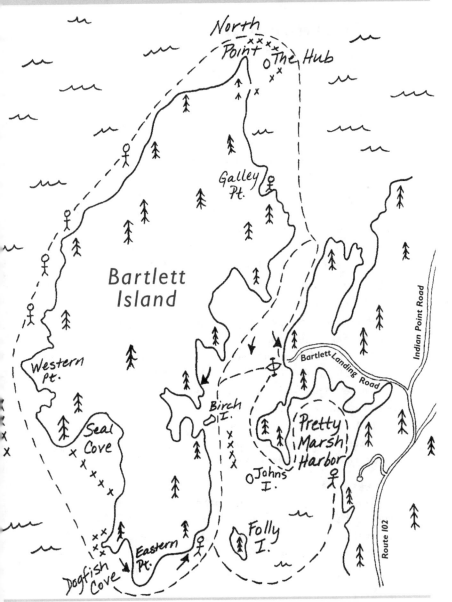

North
Point
The Hub
Galley
Pt.

Bartlett
Island

Western
Pt.

Birch
I.

Seal
Cove

Bartlett Landing Road

Pretty
Marsh
Harbor

Indian Point Road

Johns
I.

Folly
I.

Route 102

Dogfish
Cove

Eastern
Pt.

BLUE HILL BAY

water access | x x caution | landing site | point of interest | paddle trip

Bartlett Narrows

DIFFICULTY LEVEL

Beginner.

AVERAGE TRIP LENGTH

4.5–6.5 nautical miles

PADDLE SUMMARY

The Bartlett Narrows trip meets the needs of a variety of paddlers. It is a wonderful beginner trip, given its short length and protection from the wind, and a good alternative route when winds prevent more exposed trips. It is an excellent choice if you are seeking a short morning or sunset paddle. Due to its variety of wildlife and geology, it is an ideal classroom in which you can study natural history from your boat. It is also a pleasant addition to the Seal Cove trip.

ITEMS OF INTEREST

HISTORY—Bartlett Island was one of the first island settlements in the area (1767). Today, you can see the current occupation and workings of the Bartlett Farm.

GEOLOGY—Coarse-grained granite and the bedrock Ellsworth schist occur on the shore of Bartlett Island. The Pretty Marsh picnic area shoreline has boulders of almost every rock type found on Mount Desert Island.

ECOLOGY—Many animals feed within the narrows, including seals, porpoises, eagles, osprey, and loons. The granite shore of Bartlett Island has clearly banded intertidal zones.

CONDITIONS

The narrows is an ideal destination if bad weather (wind or fog) prevents paddling elsewhere. This trip can be undertaken in moderate to strong winds (10 to 15 knots) from almost any direction due to the area's extensive protection. Avoid times when the tide is running the strongest because of the current that funnels through the narrows.

ACCESS

BARTLETT ISLAND LANDING—Turn onto Indian Point Rd., heading

toward the town of Pretty Marsh (not the Pretty Marsh picnic area). Take the left fork onto Bartlett Landing Rd. Note: a town ordinance is currently under review to restrict parking at the boat landing to town residents, town taxpayers, and those renting a mooring. Check with the Mount Desert town office or a local outfitter for the current status.

SEAL COVE BOAT RAMP—Cape Rd. intersects Rte. 102 just north of Seal Cove Rd. (see Seal Cove trip).

ISLAND OWNERSHIP

JOHNS ISLAND—Maine Bureau of Public Lands.

FOLLY ISLAND—Private, monitored by the Maine Island Trail Association (MITA).

BARTLETT ISLAND—Private.

BIRCH ISLAND—Private.

LANDING SITES

BARTLETT ISLAND, ACROSS FROM FOLLY ISLAND—A protected beach with a shell midden. Very small at high tide.

PRETTY MARSH PICNIC AREA—A beautiful place to stop within Acadia National Park, with picnic tables and walking trails through the pine forest.

DO NOT LAND: Folly Island—The owners have requested that only members of the Maine Island Trail Association use this island, and for day use only. Please respect these restrictions.

CAUTION AREAS

BARTLETT NARROWS—A swift tidal current (approximately 2 knots) can occur here. Be sure to either run with the current or paddle close to the shoreline using current eddies. There is also boat traffic, including working lobster boats, the Bartlett barge, and pleasure craft. Yield the right-of-way.

THE PADDLE

Starting from either the Bartlett Island Landing or continuing from the Seal Cove paddle trip, the narrows is an easy and protected yet beautiful area full of geologic and ecological variety. This paddle description begins at the Bartlett Island landing and proceeds in a counterclockwise direction within the narrows.

Leaving the boat ramp, watch for boat traffic. This is a working harbor; yield the right-of-way to all other vessels. The view up and down the narrows is breathtaking, particularly if there is any weather or fog. Oftentimes fog banks are deflected or altered by the islands, creating unusual shapes. Due west is Bartlett Island, where you will see a dock, a blue barge, and possibly cattle grazing in the fields.

From the boat ramp, turn right, or north, and follow the Mount Desert Island shoreline. I often find big starfish and urchins here. Once you begin to leave the narrows, at about the gazebo, head across toward Bartlett Island and turn southward to explore this mussel-covered shoreline. Soon you will come abreast of the Bartlett Farm, which is owned by the Rockefeller family. This is a working farm with somewhat unusual livestock: Simmental cattle. This ancient breed of yellowish-brown and red animals originated in Switzerland, where they were bred for dairy and meat production and for draft work.

Bartlett Island is one of the most durable island communities along the coast because of the location (at the head of the Union River), the fertile soil (which is a rarity for the Maine coast due to glaciation), and the prolific and talented Bartlett clan. When the first settler arrived in 1767, there were fewer than twenty-four other families on Mount Desert Island, making Bartlett Island one of the first European settlements in this area. Although originally known as Hog Island, the settlement was quickly dominated by Bartletts; by 1790, there were eighteen family members, and by 1820 there were forty. By 1850, three-fourths of the island's 100 residents were direct descendants of the original Bartletts.

Like Ironbound Island in Frenchman Bay, Bartlett has rich soil. The Bartlett community survived primarily by farming, a livelihood very atypical of other island communities. In 1850, there were twenty-five milking cows on the island in addition to almost 200 sheep, and a yoke of oxen for each farm. Fishing was also important—understandably so, given Bartlett's access to open waters and mainland towns. There were six master mariners from the island, five of whom were Bartlett descendants. Granite and quarrying were never as profitable as on other islands, though there was a small silver rush in 1880.

At the turn of the century, the same time that there was a general mass exodus from islands to mainland towns, Bartlett too, began to disassemble. The absence of a store, church, and post office—services that add to island cohesiveness—also caused many individuals and families to move off the island to nearby Pretty Marsh.

In the early 1970s, a developer arrived on Bartlett with big plans. The Rockefeller family bought the island in 1973 to prevent a proposed island-wide development project that would have included hotels, restaurants, shops, and a bridge from the boat ramp to the Bartlett Island dock. Now the island is protected by a conservation easement held by the town of Mount Desert. The easement allows the island to be used only for private homes and farming; there will never be more than twenty-five houses, the original maximum. Currently, old fields and fences and three homes have been restored. (The act of purchasing land to avoid development is the foundation of the preserved beauty throughout this area. It was wealthy rusticators who, at the turn of the century, bought land on Mount Desert Island and created Lafayette National Park in 1916. Now called Acadia National Park, it is the only park in the country where most of the land was bought by private individuals and given to the federal government.)

(See "Geology," p. 95 and "Marine Ecology," p. 109.) The eastern shoreline of Bartlett Island south of the Bartlett Farm is Cadillac Mountain granite, which is pink and the most coarsely grained of the three granite types in the Mount Desert Island area. The granite shores are steep, and during low tide the zones of the intertidal world are accented by the bright pink background. This is one of my favorite examples of the intertidal zones, particularly heading southward along the shore toward Eastern Point. From high to low on the shore, note the black zone, followed by the barnacle zone, which blends into the rockweed zone.

(See "Social History," p. 135 and "Environmental Kayaking," p. 146.) There is abundant wildlife within the narrows. This passage is rich with fish, attracting seals, porpoises, and birds such as osprey, eagles, and terns. I also frequently see gulls, cormorants, and loons here. Continuing southward, you will see a beach on Bartlett directly across from Folly Island. Behind the beach and up the hill is a shell midden, or, more simply, a Native American garbage dump. Shell middens are used by archaeologists to research past native cultures. The shells prevent the decay of organic material in the soil. Please do not dig in or disturb the midden in any manner.

The first known owners of Folly Island were David and Isaac Bartlett. They eventually sold the island to the Somes family of Somesville. During the mid 1800s, Folly had a house with five rooms, a well, and a smokehouse. Sheep grazed the island and oats were planted—quite a lot of activity for such a little island. Folly Island is on the Maine Island Trail, a system of islands that extends for 325 miles along the coast of Maine. Only members of the Maine Island Trail Association have permission from the owners to stop on Folly Island, and only during the day.

(See "Geology," p. 95.) Continuing along Bartlett Island, the shoreline takes a direct turn westward. At this point, be sure to note the glacial erratic on the shore. This rock is Ellsworth schist; streaks of quartz and feldspar weave through the stone, giving it the appearance of marble cake. The rock is clearly metamorphosed, and it's my favorite erratic because it is so striking compared to its pink granite neighbors.

From this erratic, turn back eastward and head across the mouth of Bartlett Narrows toward Mount Desert Island. (If you are making the Bartlett Island circumnavigation trip, do not turn eastward here; instead head westward to Dogfish Cove—refer back to the original trip summary.) The crossing is approximately three-fourths of a mile. Take in the view of Western Mountain, consisting of Bernard Mountain and Mansell Mountain, part of Acadia National Park.

(See "Geology," p. 95.) The western shore of Mount Desert Island is predominantly gabbro-diorite, an intrusive dark-colored rock. Heading northward into the heart of Pretty Marsh Harbor, take time to explore the coves and inlets of this intricate shoreline. In approximately one-half to one mile, you will see a set of stairs coming down to the water. This is the Pretty Marsh picnic area, part of Acadia National Park. It is a pleasant place to stop, offering several picnic tables and short trails leading through the pine forest. Along the shore, just below the stairs, are boulders representing just about every rock type known on the island. See if you can find examples of each bedrock—Bar Harbor formation, Ellsworth schist, and Cranberry Island series—as well as the intrusive granites and gabbro-diorite.

Paddling one-half mile north from the picnic area, you will see the entrance to a small cove accessible only at high tide. This is a fun side trip that takes only a few minutes.

As you round West Point, which separates Pretty Marsh Harbor from the narrows, you are approximately one-half mile from the put-in at the Bartlett Island landing.

Bartlett Island

DIFFICULTY LEVEL
Intermediate, due to length.

AVERAGE TRIP LENGTH
8 nautical miles.

PADDLE SUMMARY
The circumnavigation of Bartlett Island is a rewarding full-day trip of geological interest and frequent wildlife sightings. Bartlett Island itself has a long history and is still occupied. *(See the Blue Hill Bay chart on p. 55.)*

ITEMS OF INTEREST
HISTORY—Bartlett Island was one of the first island settlements in the area (1767). Today, you can see the current occupation and workings of the Bartlett Farm.

GEOLOGY—Perfect examples of coarse-grained granite and the bedrock Ellsworth schist, also glacial erratics and dramatic cliffs.

ECOLOGY—Many seals and porpoises feed in this area, as do eagles and osprey. The granite shore of Bartlett Island has clearly banded intertidal zones. Bartlett Island itself is home to a herd of Simmental cattle.

CONDITIONS
This trip is best taken in winds up to moderate strength (0–15 knots). The west side is exposed; while on the east side, you will be paddling into a headwind.

ACCESS
BARTLETT ISLAND LANDING—Turn onto Indian Point Rd., heading toward the town of Pretty Marsh (not the Pretty Marsh picnic area).

Take the left fork at the Downtown Pretty Marsh sign onto Bartlett Landing Rd. Note: a town ordinance is currently under review to restrict parking at the boat landing to town residents, town taxpayers, and those renting a mooring. Check with the Mount Desert town office or a local outfitter for the current status.

ISLAND OWNERSHIP

BARTLETT ISLAND—Private.

THE HUB—Maine Bureau of Public Lands, monitored by the Maine Island Trail Association (MITA).

LANDING SITES

There are many beaches all along Bartlett Island's shoreline. The owners have posted that day visitors are welcome, but please no fires or camping.

DO NOT LAND: Seal Cove, at the southwest corner of Bartlett Island (seal colony), or The Hub (seal haul-out area). Refer to "Environmental Kayaking," p. 146.

CAUTION AREAS

BARTLETT NARROWS—A swift tidal current (approximately 2 knots) can occur here. Be sure to either run with this current or paddle close to the shoreline using current eddies. There is also boat traffic, including working lobster boats, the Bartlett barge, and pleasure craft. Yield the right-of-way.

BARTLETT ISLAND, WEST SIDE—The west side of Bartlett is quite open and exposed; be careful of winds and swells.

THE PADDLE

The circumnavigation, be it clockwise or counterclockwise, should be decided by the wind direction on the day you plan to make your trip. The most exposed leg of the paddle is the west side of the island, where you'll want to have the wind at your back. This paddle description proceeds in a clockwise direction, assuming the wind direction is southwest.

The first leg of the trip, within the Bartlett Island Narrows, is described on pages 56–61. Do not, however, begin paddling north as is suggested there; instead, immediately cross over to Bartlett Island and proceed south from the Bartlett Farm.

From the glacial erratic, turn westward toward Eastern Point, the southernmost point of Bartlett. Immediately after the point is Dogfish Cove, one of my preferred lunch spots. The large beach in the cove offers beautiful views of Hardwood Island and greater Blue Hill Bay. The steep eastern cliffs here are made up of a small band of gabbro-diorite, while the western side marks the transition to Ellsworth schist, which forms the entire west side of Bartlett Island.

At low tide, the rockweed clings to the rock overhangs on the right side of the cove. I love to paddle here, within the rock-

Dogfish Cove.
W. DAVID ANDREWS II.

weed-clad "cave," looking at the many starfish, mussels, and urchins.

(See "Environmental Kayaking," p. 146.) On Dogfish Point there are nesting osprey. Stay well offshore so as not to disturb them, especially in spring when there are young chicks. On the same note, as you turn north, do not enter Seal Cove; a seal colony lives here. Disturbance from sea kayakers can be very detrimental to them. Because these seals are in a cove rather than on open ledges, they have fewer escape routes and therefore are more easily panicked by approaching boats.

Following this shoreline for the next four nautical miles, you will be in the open waters of Blue Hill Bay. There are numerous beaches to stop on along this shoreline.

To the left, or west, is Long Island, which is worthy of mention. At four and a half miles long and two miles wide, it is by far the largest

Long Island as seen from Hardwood Island.
W. DAVID ANDREWS II.

island in Blue Hill Bay. The first settlers, Ebenezer Hinckley and James Candage, arrived in 1768. Their sawmill, named "Improvement," did not last long, for Hinckley was found frozen to death in March 1776. The island was eventually settled, and a school opened in 1880 with thirty students. A post office operated from 1890 to 1903, and there was a dance hall in 1910. Many families left soon after the turn of the century; the island was no longer inhabited by humans after 1920.

A lawyer and huntsman named Frank Sibley eventually bought the island with the goal of creating a game preserve. A fence was built across the island in an effort to limit the game to the north end. This was soon proven ineffective, and the entire idea was eventually abandoned. The island was then used for blueberry farming, which was quite successful. To prevent unwanted growth and to enrich the soil, the island was deliberately burned several times.

A local story tells of a poker game between two owners of Long Island who strongly disliked each other. The winner placed American bison on the island to prevent the other from using it. Colorful, yes; true, no. The current owner of the island explains that while it is true that there were buffalo on the island, they were brought there to control vegetation so that the island could be used for recreation.

Much of Long Island is subject to a conservation easement held by Acadia National Park. The easement guarantees that 97 percent of this island will remain in a "forever wild" state. The buffalo were removed in the summer of 1997. (I still remember the first time I encountered the animals. A group of us were on the shore calmly eating our lunch when we heard a noise and looked up to see eight huge shadows rounding the corner and slowly walking toward us. I got on my radio and called my outfitter. "What should I do if they start charging?" I stuttered. Within a background of laughter, I was advised, "Take away their credit card.")

(See "Environmental Kayaking," p. 146.) Back at Bartlett Island, heading north, you will eventually round North Point and come upon The Hub. This little island is owned by the state and is part of the Maine Island Trail, a system of islands that extends from Casco Bay to Machias Bay. The Hub has, at various times, also been home to a seal colony with pups in the spring. If you are paddling between late April and late

June, or if seals are hauled out, give the island an extremely wide berth to avoid disturbing them.

The shoreline back into the narrows becomes granite again around Galley Point, which has a very pleasant beach. You may choose instead to cross over to the Mount Desert Island shoreline of gabbro-diorite and follow it back to the boat ramp. The view all the way down the narrows and into Blue Hill Bay is breathtaking.

Seal Cove

DIFFICULTY LEVEL
Beginner/Intermediate.

AVERAGE TRIP LENGTH
4–8 nautical miles.

PADDLE SUMMARY
Seal Cove is the most direct access point to Blue Hill Bay, complete with parking and a boat ramp, beach, and picnic area. Spend a portion of the day paddling north past Moose and Hardwood Islands while watching for osprey, eagles, seals, and porpoises. The trip can be extended by visiting Dogfish Cove on Bartlett Island or exploring Bartlett Narrows and Pretty Marsh Harbor.

ITEMS OF INTEREST
HISTORY—Hardwood Island is currently occupied during the summer. Beautiful views abound of Bartlett Narrows, Blue Hill Bay, and Western Mountain in Acadia National Park.

GEOLOGY—Bedrock Ellsworth schist and gabbro-diorite.

ECOLOGY—Many seals and porpoises feed here, as do a large number and variety of birds. Aquaculture farm pens can be observed.

CONDITIONS
This paddle can be undertaken in light to moderate winds (0–15 knots). Because there is little commercial boat traffic, this trip is also suitable for foggy days.

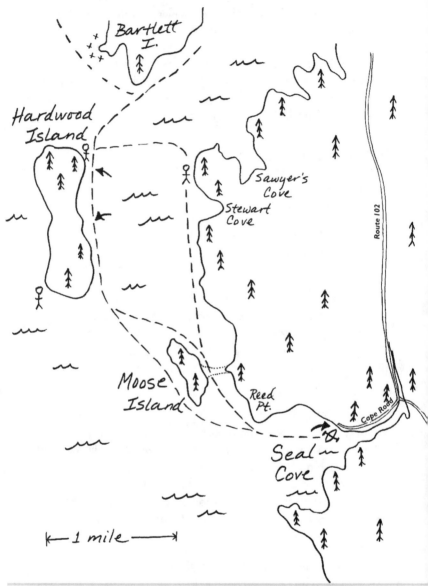

Bartlett I.

Hardwood Island

Sawyer's Cove

Stewart Cove

Route 102

Moose Island

Reed Pt.

Cape Road

Seal Cove

←— 1 mile —→

BLUE HILL BAY, SOUTH OF BARTLETT ISLAND

water access   caution   landing site   point of interest   paddle trip

ACCESS

SEAL COVE BOAT RAMP—Cape Rd. intersects Rte. 102 just north of Seal Cove Rd.

ISLAND OWNERSHIP

MOOSE—Private.

HARDWOOD—Private.

LANDING SITES

HARDWOOD, SOUTHERN TIP—A huge beach, good at any tide. (Away from private residences.)

HARDWOOD, NORTHEAST TIP—Good beach at three-fourths tide and lower. (Away from private residences.)

NORTHERN END OF STEWART COVE—A small beach known locally as Chuck's Cove. Beach is very small at high tide. (Note: Stewart Cove is not labeled on all charts. It is one-half mile south of Sawyer's Cove.)

DO NOT LAND: Moose Island—The owners, who live in the gray house across from the island, request that boaters do not land.

CAUTION AREAS

Be aware of working lobster boats; give them a wide berth.

THE PADDLE

(See "Geology," p. 95.) Before leaving Seal Cove, take a look at the shoreline. This marbled rock is a pocket of Ellsworth schist, a metamorphic bedrock, within a larger mass of jumbled contact zone. The contact zone, or shatter zone, appears as a haphazard mixture of different types of rocks.

Paddling out of the cove, you will see Reed Point on the right. From here, turn northward and you will see a view I often visit in my dreams: Moose, Hardwood, and Bartlett Islands, partially bordered by Mount Desert Island. It is a quintessential example of Maine scenery.

You can pass Moose Island on either the west or east side, although for two and a half hours before and after low tide a bar is exposed between the gray house and the island. Cross closer to the island out of respect for the homeowners; you are paddling in their front yard.

Cattle were kept on Moose Island during its settlement in the early 1800s and were driven across the bar daily because of the lack of fresh water on the island. I often thought the island should have been named Cow Island until the summer of 1995, when a moose actually was seen here. Be sure to explore the wonderfully complicated and jumbled shoreline of Moose Island. The southern tip is the bedrock Ellsworth schist, formed 450 million years ago; the rest of the island consists of contact zone rocks.

Entering the waters between Hardwood, Moose, and Bartlett Islands, you can easily imagine the days when this part of the bay was filled with ships, captained and crewed by the men from the islands, on their way to trade goods with Boston and beyond. (I remember one foggy day when a huge wooden gaff-rigged schooner sailed by—I had heard it coming because of the bagpiper playing on deck.) This bay, at the mouth of Bartlett Narrows, is frequently visited by seals and porpoises attracted by the fish funneling through the narrows. Also watch for osprey and bald eagles, loons, cormorants, and gulls, which live and feed in this area.

Northwest of Moose Island is Hardwood Island, whose name aptly

This beach is a great landing spot on the southern side of Hardwood Island.
W. DAVID ANDREWS II.

describes its unusual forest cover. It is one of the few islands that have not been logged extensively. The resulting mix of oak, maple, and beech trees at the northern end is distinct from the more common island spruce and fir forests that grow today on previously cleared land. Known in the past as Beach, Bear, or My Island, Hardwood received its current name around 1820.

On the southern end of Hardwood Island is a beautiful, long cobble beach with rock outcroppings. Please stay below the high-tide mark, as there is a fragile marsh with duck nesting boxes just behind the beach-pea-covered dunes. Currently, there is a biological station, run by the Cleveland Museum of Natural History, that hosts an eight-week summer ecology camp for high-school students. The buildings you see are part of this camp. Also on the east side is an aquaculture farm that raises Atlantic salmon for use in restaurants. These pens are a fun place to watch the fish as they jump high into the air, as if they were ascending rapids on their way to spawn.

On the northeastern end of Hardwood is a beach that is accessible at three-fourths tide and lower. The island is mostly gabbro-diorite except for the southwestern tip, which is of Ellsworth schist.

From Hardwood, you may choose to visit Bartlett Island by exploring Dogfish Cove or paddling up into Bartlett Narrows (be sure to refer to the Bartlett Narrows paddle trip, page 56). Otherwise, cross over to the shoreline of Mount Desert Island, where there is a little beach, known locally as Chuck's Cove, on the northern edge of Stewart Cove (see note under Landing Sites, above). The nearby rocks are striped with quartz veins. From here, you can explore the contact zone shoreline as you paddle back south to Seal Cove.

The Cranberry Isles

These islands, just south of Mount Desert Island, offer an array of paddling trips, from a quick jaunt after work to a full-day excursion. The area has a variety of geologic wonders and wildlife, and a long, rich history of human settlement colored by several well-known coastal characters.

The Cranberry Isles, which include Baker, Bear, Sutton, Great Cranberry, and Little Cranberry Islands, are named after the 200-acre bog on Great Cranberry Island. The bog was once drained to curtail the mosquito population, but, as one local put it, "The mosquitoes came back, but the cranberries didn't."

The Cranberry Isles were settled around the time of the American Revolution, and by 1800 there were fourteen or fifteen households totaling 125 residents. In 1830, when the town of Cranberry Isles became incorporated, there were thirty-seven families among the five islands, totaling 170 people. It remains today a separate township. Currently, the year-round population is 160 people split between Great and Little Cranberry; there are no year-round residents on Baker, Sutton, or Bear Islands. The summer population of Little and Great Cranberry totals 700.

Little and Great Cranberry have played an important role as fishing and shipping stations because of their established communities and their favorable location at the entrance of Somes Sound, Southwest Harbor, and Northeast harbor.

When planning a paddling trip, you can choose among several put-in sites, all described below. Then, continue on your choice of paddling trips, which are described in the following sections. These are the most favorable routes based on weather considerations and items of interest, but feel free to tailor any trip to best meet your needs. The first one, Inner Cranberry Islands, covers mostly the inner waters of Eastern Way and the Mount Desert shoreline. The second trip, Outer Cranberry Islands, is an advanced excursion that proceeds around Little Cranberry, with an alternative route for poor weather.

ACCESS

SOUTHWEST HARBOR—Turn onto Clark Point Rd. from the blinking light in the center of town. At the fork in the road, continue following Clark Point Rd. to the right. This will lead you to the Mount Desert Oceanarium (a great place to learn about marine ecology), Beal's Lobster Pier, the Coast Guard station, and the boat ramp. Parking is limited here to three hours, except for a few eight-hour spaces up on the rock wall to the right of the ramp. These are used by fishermen.

MANSET—South of the center of Southwest Harbor, turn onto Rte. 102A toward the Seawall Campground. Turn onto Mansell Ln. at the Double J grocery and deli. At the road's end, take a left onto the Shore Rd. (to the right is the Hinckley boat yard). Just down the street is the public boat ramp. This shoreline has a small isolated patch of the bedrock Bar Harbor formation, a layered sedimentary rock.

SEAL HARBOR—The beach and parking lot are located off Rte. 3 in the town of Seal Harbor. This harbor has one of only two sand beaches on the island. At high tide, you will have to carry your boats only twenty to thirty feet. At low tide, the beach extends quite far out, and the carry can be quite a haul.

Despite having to time your put-in with the tides, Seal Harbor is one of my favorite places for launching. The protected sand beach, enclosed in a huge cove, is easy on boats, and the sights are breathtaking. You can pass among the mostly pleasure boats that moor here.

As you paddle out toward green can #1, scan the shoreline and hills for spectacular houses. One-half mile from the beach is Crowninshield Point. Take a moment to examine the huge house here. The flagpole can be a good point of reference.

NORTHEAST HARBOR—The town dock is to the east of Main St. Any number of roads extending from town to the left can take you there.

The public boat ramp next to the Northeast Harbor town dock is a pleasant and easy put-in site with restrooms nearby.

The western shoreline of Northeast Harbor is made up of contact zone rock, a jumble of many different bedrock types. It is interesting to see, particularly at lower tides. There are several large, impressive houses on the shore; Northeast Harbor is a well-to-do community. As you come to the entrance of the harbor, the shoreline becomes Bar Harbor formation, which is mostly found in Frenchman Bay. This layered sedimentary bedrock is often brown or rust in color.

CAUTION AREAS

MANSET AND SOUTHWEST HARBOR—Both put-in sites flank a working harbor that includes a Coast Guard station. Many boats enter and leave the area, and the boat traffic can be heavy. Stay out of these areas in fog, for kayaks are not clearly detected by radar.

WESTERN WAY—This major entrance to Southwest and Northeast Harbors is used by large vessels, and boat traffic can be heavy. During the summer, many boat races occur here. Use extreme caution.

NORTHEAST HARBOR—Stay close to shore, out of the major channel, leaving room for the larger boats that must use this narrow harbor entrance.

EASTERN WAY—This is also a major entrance into the area. Use extreme caution when crossing this channel, especially in fog.

CROWNINSHIELD POINT, SEAL HARBOR—There are several shallow rocks that are exposed at low tide. At higher water levels, a breaking wave is sometimes created by the submerged ledge.

EAST BUNKER LEDGE—Large waves can develop here. Please stay away because of the seal population. Refer to "Environmental Kayaking," p. 146.

BAKER ISLAND BAR—Breaking waves and strong current can occur here. Avoid this area when the tide and wind oppose each other.

CRANBERRY HARBOR—This area has heavy working-boat traffic, including the ferry service.

Inner Cranberry Islands

DIFFICULTY

Beginner/Intermediate.

AVERAGE TRIP LENGTH

Up to 11 nautical miles, depending on put-in and chosen route.

PADDLE SUMMARY

The Inner Cranberry Islands route is a beautiful paddle that can easily be modified. From any one of a number of put-in sites, this paddling trip follows the southern shoreline of Mount Desert Island and offers a variety of geologic features, a high probability of both harbor seal and gray seal sightings, and wonderful views of Little and Great Cranberry Islands. This paddle, although rated beginner/intermediate, is in fairly open waters, allowing a sensation of the raw ocean.

ITEMS OF INTEREST

HISTORY—Greening Island was bought from the Native Americans for one gallon of rum. The Bear Island Lighthouse was built in 1838.

GEOLOGY—Granite, cobblestone beaches, and examples of the bedrock Bar Harbor formation and contact zone shorelines.

ECOLOGY—You're likely to see not only harbor seals, but also the less common gray seal. Many birds, including cormorants, gulls, loons, terns, bald eagles, and osprey, are often sighted in this area.

CONDITIONS

Paddle this trip only in light to moderate winds (0–15 knots). Winds from the southwest or north are fine, but avoid the area in an east wind, for there is no protection. Additionally, the south side of Mount Desert Island is very foggy, and the fog banks can roll in quickly, often without warning.

ACCESS

See page 71.

ISLAND OWNERSHIP

GREENING ISLAND—Private.
BEAR ISLAND—Private.

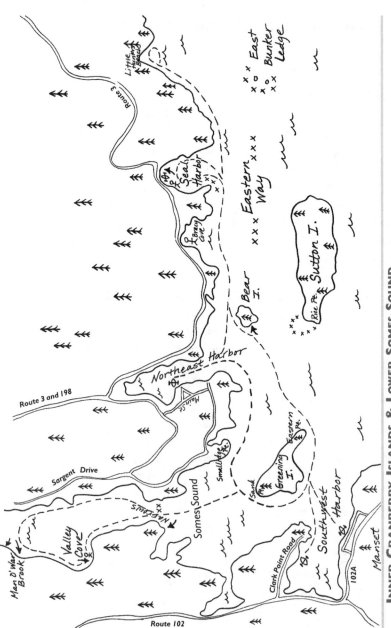

Route 3

Little Hunters Beach

East Bunker Ledge

Seal Harbor

Eastern Way

Bracy Cove

Sutton I.

Rice Pt.

Bear I.

Northeast Harbor

Route 3 and 198

Main St.

Sargent Drive

Smallidge Pt.

Eastern Pt.

Greening I.

Spunk

Narrows

Somes Sound

Man O'War Brook

Valley Cove

Southwest Harbor

Clark Point Road

Mansett

102A

Route 102

INNER CRANBERRY ISLANDS & LOWER SOMES SOUND

water　×× caution　♀ landing　➤ point of　⌢⌣ paddle

LANDING SITES

BRACY COVE—Protected. Mud from low to mid-tide, cobblestone beach from mid- to high tide.

SEAL HARBOR—Large protected sand beach.

CAUTION AREAS

See p. 72.

THE PADDLE

The put-in sites for this paddle are described in the Cranberry Isles introduction. This route description begins at Northeast Harbor, however, you may design or modify your own trip.

From Northeast Harbor, paddle west. Watch for the ledge between the cans that mark the harbor entrance. The shoreline along here is entirely Bar Harbor formation. Passing Sargent Head, watch for the orange day markers that indicate a large ledge; there are often many birds here.

Continuing past Smallidge Point, you will see several houses in the town of Northeast Harbor. The only locally owned shorefront property is a piece around the corner with a large working dock extending out into the water; the rest is owned by seasonal residents. Turn southwest and cross one-half mile to Greening Island, which is entirely fine-grained granite.

(See "Social History," p. 135.) This island was bought by Abraham Somes in 1755 from the Abenaki Indians who lived in the area. The price: one gallon of rum. In 1837, James Greenan moved onto and eventually owned the entire island. It was probably then that the island was named Greening. In the late 1800s, Greening had a 9-hole golf course. Descendants of several of the original families still summer here.

From the western shore, you can see all the way up Somes Sound to the north and spot busy Southwest Harbor to the west. From the south side, you can see directly out into the open ocean. You can also see Great Cranberry in the foreground and Little Cranberry in the background. To the east is Sutton Island.

Leaving Eastern Point, use caution crossing Western Way toward Bear Island. This is a major thoroughfare and heavy with both working- and recreational-boat traffic. The crossing is approximately one mile long.

From the western shore of Bear Island, look at the cliff and caves created by the impact of the open sea upon a shoreline of Bar Harbor formation. This type of erosion can also be seen along the Shore Route and Long Porcupine Island in Frenchman Bay and The Ovens in Mount Desert Narrows.

Bear Island was farmed, logged, and used for sheep pasturage. The lighthouse on the island was originally built in 1838, and in 1840 a keeper and his family of five moved onto the island. By 1856, there were two families and a small school. The lighthouse was replaced by a lighted bell buoy in 1981. After 142 years, the island was vacated and is now occupied only during the summer by descendants of the family who

Bear Island Lighthouse.
W. DAVID ANDREWS II.

originally bought the island in 1884 and by the inhabitants of the lighthouse, which is currently owned by the national park and leased out as a private residence.

(See "Geology," p. 95.) Cross over to Mount Desert Island to the north; the shoreline here is a small outcropping of gabbro-diorite, the only such exposure on the southern half of Mount Desert Island. The most abundant gabbro-diorite outcroppings can be seen on the Porcupine Islands in Frenchman Bay and on the Seal Cove trip in Blue Hill Bay.

(See "Geology," p. 95.) Continuing to the east, the shore turns inland and forms Bracy Cove. This is a pleasant beach for stopping. The shoreline forming the entrance to the cove is contact zone rocks, similar to those of Northeast Harbor. This a wonderful shoreline to examine for its variety and uniqueness; it seems as though no two rocks are alike.

(See "Geology," p. 95.) Before coming to Crowninshield Point, be sure to read the put-in site description for Seal Harbor (page 71). It is a pretty cove to explore, with its many sailing boats and one of the finest beaches to stop on for lunch. The shoreline, particularly the eastern one, is a clear example of coarse-grained Cadillac Mountain granite.

Leaving Seal Harbor, you may either return to your original launching site or continue east toward Little Hunter's Beach, though I do not recommend attempting to land here. The paddle to Little Hunter's Beach is open and exposed, offering views of endless ocean and some of the choice luxury houses of Seal Harbor.

Outer Cranberry Islands

DIFFICULTY LEVEL

Advanced, due to exposure. (An intermediate trip or poor-weather alternative trip is included.)

AVERAGE TRIP LENGTH

CIRCUMNAVIGATION OF LITTLE CRANBERRY

8.5–10.5 nautical miles.

INNER CRANBERRY HARBOR

6–8 nautical miles.

PADDLE SUMMARY

The Outer Cranberry Islands route is an exciting and exposed trip offering year-round communities, a museum, and artist galleries. This is a wonderful choice for those seeking rare volcanic geology, grand views of Mount Desert Island, and highly probable wildlife sightings. Offering little protection from the open ocean, this route should be attempted only by advanced paddlers.

ITEMS OF INTEREST

HISTORY—Bear Island Lighthouse, built in 1838, and Sutton Island, the home of John Gilley and author Rachel Field. The town of Islesford and Great Cranberry, both year-round island communities, can be visited. Baker Island was the home of William Gilley.

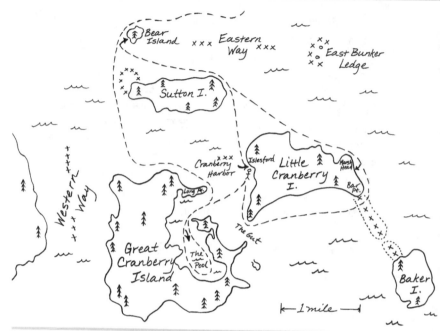

OUTER CRANBERRY ISLANDS

⊠ water access   x x x caution   ⚕ landing site   ⬎ point of interest   ⌒⌒ paddle trip

GEOLOGY—Seal Harbor has one of two sand beaches on Mount Desert Island. You'll see the bedrock Bar Harbor formation, Cranberry Island series, contact zone shorelines, and granite.

ECOLOGY—Harbor seals are frequent, in addition to the less common gray seal. An osprey nest reported to be more than 100 years old exists on Sutton Island. The Pool is a shallow, protected bay nestled within Grant Cranberry.

CONDITIONS

This trip is for advanced paddlers only. Paddle only in light to moderate winds (0–15 knots) for the inner harbor trip, and light winds (0–10) knots for the outer island trip. Winds from the southwest or north are fine, but do not paddle in an east wind, for there is no protection. In addition, the south side of Mount Desert Island is very foggy, and the fog banks roll in quickly, often without warning.

ACCESS

See p. 71.

ISLAND OWNERSHIP

BEAR ISLAND—Private.

SUTTON ISLAND—Private.

LITTLE CRANBERRY—Public/private.

GREAT CRANBERRY—Public/private.

LANDING SITES

LITTLE CRANBERRY—There are numerous beaches around the island; please respect private property. There is a pebble beach to either side of the town dock in the village of Islesford.

GREAT CRANBERRY—There are many beaches around the island; please respect private property.

CAUTION SITES

See p. 72.

THE PADDLE

Put-in sites for this paddle are described in the Cranberry Isles introduction. If you put in at Northeast Harbor, watch for the ledge between the cans at the entrance to the harbor as you head toward Bear Island. If you launch from Seal Harbor, you may chose to follow the shoreline to the west toward Bear Island and paddle in a generally counterclockwise direction; if you head directly out toward Little Cranberry, your trip will be in a clockwise direction. This paddle trip proceeds in a counterclockwise direction from Bear Island for ease of incorporating all the put-in sites.

(See "Geology," p. 95.) Bear Island is a small yet beautifully dramatic island. There are obviously no bears on the island; the name most likely was Bare originally, because of its rocky shores. Made entirely of the bedrock Bar Harbor formation, the island is tall and steep (eighty feet) with impressive cliffs and caves on the western shore. (For more about this charming island, see p. 76 in the Inner Cranberry Islands route description.)

(See "Marine Ecology," p. 109 and "Environmental Kayaking," p. 146.) Continue southward toward Sutton Island. On the northwesternmost corner of the island is one of the oldest known osprey nests in the area. It has been occupied for more than 100 years. Stay at least one-fourth of a mile from the nest (half the channel width). These birds experience a great level of disturbance nesting in this high-traffic area. During the summer months in particular, osprey are laying eggs

Osprey nest on Sutton Island.
(Note: this photo was taken with a telephoto lens; paddlers should not approach nests this closely.)
W. DAVID ANDREWS II.

and raising young. This is a critical time of year for them, and your co-operation can make a big difference in their survival.

Also located on Sutton Island are rare Leach's storm-petrels. About the size of swallows, they are nocturnal and therefore seldom seen (I have yet to spot one). Mariners consider a sighting of a storm petrel lucky because they are an early warning sign of an upcoming storm.

(See "Social History," p. 135.) Sutton Island has an interesting history. In 1755, Eben Sutton, who was settling the area with Abraham Somes, bought the island from the Abenaki Indians for two quarts of rum. Although the island remained unoccupied until 1830, it eventually had its own school, which was open until 1920, and a post office until 1947. Sutton had one of the first island telephones—one line for all eight houses, each one having its own ring.

One famous resident was John Gilley, who lived here from 1850 to 1896 and sold produce, dairy products, and fish to the summer people in the area. He also had a pogy press and dealt in real estate. Impressed with this man, Charles Eliot, president of Harvard University, wrote a book about him in 1904 called *John Gilley: Maine Farmer and Fisherman.* The book is still read today, under the new title *John Gilley, One of the Forgotten Millions.* Another well-known Sutton personality was author Rachel Field, who wrote children's books, novels, and poetry.

Around the turn of the century, more and more summer people and vacationers began to buy property on the island, and those who remained year-round went from farming and fishing to caretaking. Property prices increased, encouraging locals to sell. Because the children of local families could no longer establish homes on the island, Sutton's native community eventually ceased to exist. Today, Sutton Island is owned entirely by people "from away" and is occupied only during the summer.

The fate of this island raises issues that are being grappled with by many other Maine island towns and coastal communities, including Mount Desert Island. Permanent communities are hard to maintain when too high a percentage of the land is used for vacation homes.

The north and south shores of Sutton Island are beautiful, and it is worth planning your trip so as to see both. The south side has a gravel shore with a large gravel bar called Rice Point. The north shore is laced with caves and arches within tall cliffs of fine-grained granite.

At this point, you need to decide whether to stay within Cranberry Harbor—which is recommended if you are an intermediate paddler or if the wind is strong—or whether to circumnavigate Little Cranberry, which is an option if you are an expert paddler, the winds are light (0–10 knots), and the weather is favorable. Be aware that at low tide the Baker

The author paddling under an arch on Sutton Island.
W. DAVID ANDREWS II.

Eastern Way

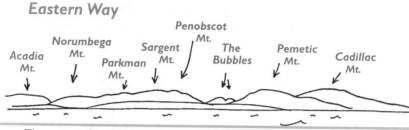

The mountains of Acadia as seen from the Cranberry Islands.

Island Bar, at the southeastern tip of Little Cranberry, is fully exposed, and you may have to paddle almost to Baker Island before crossing over. The following describes the circumnavigation, then the inner harbor trip.

ISLAND CIRCUMNAVIGATION—*(See "Geology," p. 95)* Leave Sutton Island and head toward the northern shore of Little Cranberry, watching for boat traffic. Along this shore you will see several cobblestone beaches and coves, which are fun to explore. Rounding Marsh Head, on the northeasternmost corner, you will come upon a large cobble seawall created by the unbroken exposure to the sea.

Take a moment to look at Baker Island, whose name, I always say, comes from its round cake shape with a single candle (the lighthouse) in the middle. In fact, there is no explanation of its origin; it just appeared on charts in 1760. Today, Acadia National Park runs a boat trip to the island to tell the story of William and Hannah Gilley and to explore the remaining houses and cemetery of this well-known island family.

William and Hannah Gilley settled Baker Island during the War of 1812. They lived a completely self-sufficient life, raising and growing all their own food and making most of what was required to meet their material needs. William farmed and fished while Hannah bore and educated twelve children. She rowed them all to church in Southwest Harbor, seven miles away, every summer Sunday.

In 1828, William became the first keeper of the newly built lighthouse on the island, a position he would retain for twenty-one years. As keeper, he earned $350 a year and all the sperm oil his family needed for their lamps. Having no living expenses, the Gilley family soon became financially well-off. They did not own Baker Island, but simply followed a long Maine island tradition of squatters' rights. When the Lighthouse Board bought the island from the U.S. Government, a long and heated battle for land ownership began between the government and the Gilleys.

Mr. Gilley was eventually removed as keeper in 1849 at the age of sixty-seven and transferred to nearby Great Duck Island. Baker Island remained occupied by Gilley descendants for many years, continuing the battle begun by their father. The light was automated in 1966, and the island became part of Acadia National Park.

Continuing southward, in one-half mile you will come to Bar Point and the Baker Island Bar. Use great caution here, for crossing this bar can be tricky. At low tide, the shoal is exposed and you must paddle around it. If the wind and the tidal current are opposing each other, standing waves develop. The building on Bar Point used to be a government-funded lifesaving station, which would assist vessels in need; it was a precursor to the Coast Guard.

Past the bar, on the south side of Little Cranberry, is a cobble beach approximately one mile long. Soon you will come to The Gut, the passage between Little Cranberry and Great Cranberry. This is a very tricky passageway; many vessels have run aground and sunk here. Round the point of land called The Maypole and continue along the Little Cranberry shore until you come to the town of Islesford. (Description of Islesford continues on p. 84.)

INNER HARBOR—*(See "Geology," p. 95.)* Leave Sutton Island and head toward Great Cranberry. The large dock you see on the northern shore is the town dock, where the ferries from Southwest Harbor and Northeast Harbor land. Be aware of boat traffic. The shoreline to the east is all Cranberry Island series, a volcanic rock.

Heading southeast and rounding Long Point, you will come to the entrance of The Pool, a large inlet into Great Cranberry. The entrance is shallow during low tide, so watch for exposed rocks. The town you see is Cranberry Isles. Once you've finished exploring the protected salt marsh of The Pool, cross Cranberry Harbor approximately three-fourths of a mile to the town of Islesford on Little Cranberry.

* * *

The Islesford town wharf, date unknown.
NORTHEAST HARBOR LIBRARY.

Islesford is one of my favorite places to stop. You may land on the beaches to either the left or right of the town dock. There are a restaurant and a little artist's shop on the dock. Acadia National Park has a small museum just north of the dock; its grassy lawn is a fine place to eat lunch. The museum tells the history of the Cranberry Isles, the discovery of the area, and early island life. Open from June to September (call the Park for information), the museum is well worth the visit. You may also choose to walk to the center of the island. There are several old cemeteries, a store and post office around which island life revolves, two beautiful churches, a one-room schoolhouse, and an artist's studio. A map of the island is available at the museum. Note that none of the island cars have license plates or are registered or inspected. (They also don't have mufflers.) Ah, island life!

Once you have finished exploring Islesford, you can plan your return trip to Mount Desert Island to see new sights, depending on your original put-in place.

Somes Sound

*To some persons, this Sound is the greatest wonder of all ...
nothing could be more delightful than the mornings we
spent upon its waters, floating—no whence no whither,—now
on a sea of glass, now scudding swiftly before brisk breezes,
—guiding our little boat under the birchen shadows of
the Narrows, or pausing awe struck, under the dark frown of
the cliff, while the great bald eagles sailed over our heads
and the solemn echoes rolled above the murmur of the pines.*

MRS. CLARA BARNES
*LORING, SHORT, AND HARMON'S ILLUSTRATED GUIDE BOOK
FOR MOUNT DESERT ISLAND, 4TH ED., 1877*

Cutting Mount Desert Island nearly in half, Somes Sound is the only
fjord in the eastern United States. It was carved by a giant ice sheet
15,000 to 25,000 years ago. Called the Wisconsin Glacier, the ice
scraped and sculpted Somes Sound as it did the many lakes on the
island, all running north–south. The difference is that the sound was
never completely cut off from the sea, so instead of filling with fresh water, it was filled by the ocean. The walls of this U-shaped valley are granite mountains rising to almost 1,000 feet.

Ecologically, the sound is unique because of its great depth and
small opening, which prevents a thorough water flow and mixing; it
takes many tidal cycles to change the water within the sound. The head
of Somes Sound is very protected; it is a mudflat geographically defined
by granite and conifers rather than dunes and beach grass, the more

common neighbors of a mudflat. Seals, cormorants, great blue herons, and bald eagles live in this organically rich and productive area.

Somes Sound has played a part in many historical events in this area's history, from an attempted settlement at Fernald Point that would become the first conflict between the French and English in Maine, to hideouts in Valley Cove during the many years of continued fighting for control of this area, to Abraham Somes founding Somesville—the first European settlement on Mount Desert Island. Somes Sound continues to be a special place for locals and visitors alike.

The sound is a dramatically beautiful paddling area offering many geologic, ecological, and historic wonders. The following section contains paddling trips for Lower Somes Sound and Upper Somes Sound.

Lower Somes Sound

Refer to the Inner Cranberry Islands map on p. 74

DIFFICULTY LEVEL

Beginner/Intermediate.

AVERAGE TRIP LENGTH

6–12 nautical miles, depending on put-in site.

PADDLE SUMMARY

Lower Somes Sound is a wonderful trip through a historic area. It offers the beauty of The Narrows and Valley Cove and a terrific five-mile view up the belly of Somes Sound. As you follow the shoreline to and from the sound, you'll see open and exposed views of the Cranberry Isles and nearby island harbors.

ITEMS OF INTEREST

HISTORY—Fernald Point, the site of the first conflict that would lead to the French and Indian War, and Valley Cove, where both French and English boats hid during the confrontation.

GEOLOGY—Contact-zone shoreline, Bar Harbor formation, and granite. The trip extends into the mouth of a natural fjord with steep granite mountains on each side.

ECOLOGY—Seals and many birds, including eagles and ospreys, frequent the area.

CONDITIONS

The optimal weather for this trip is light to moderate winds (0–15 knots) from the southwest. Due-north or due-south winds are usually strong due to their unbroken path up or down the sound, and they will create a headwind during one leg of the trip. Also note that you will be completely unprotected outside of the sound in a due-east wind. A very stiff current runs through The Narrows as the sound fills and empties, and kayakers will have difficulty paddling against this flow. Time your trip so you paddle through The Narrows either running with the tide or during slack tide.

ACCESS

See Cranberry Isles access, p. 71.

ISLAND OWNERSHIP

GREENING ISLAND—Private.

LANDING SITES

VALLEY COVE—A very protected cove with a long beach (completely covered at high tide). There is access to hiking trails and a road, though it is currently closed to vehicles.

CAUTION AREAS

See Cranberry Isles caution areas, p. 72.

THE PADDLE

From your put-in site, proceed to Sand Point on Greening Island.

Greening Island was bought by Abraham Somes in 1755 from the Abenaki Indians who lived in the area. The price: one gallon of rum. In 1837, James Greenan moved onto and eventually owned the entire island. It was probably then that the island was named Greening. In the late 1800s, Greening had a 9-hole golf course. Descendants of several of the original families still summer here.

Take a moment to look at your surroundings. To the west lies Southwest Harbor; to the east, Northeast Harbor. Directly north, Somes Sound divides Mount Desert Island almost in half, with Somesville at its head. For literally hundreds of years, mariners have stopped here to gaze in awe at this magnificent finger of water flanked by mountains.

(See "Social History," p. 135.) One such group decided to settle here at Fernald Point, the field to the west of The Narrows. Two French Jesuit priests, Father Biard and Father Masse, formed a colony called St. Sauveur in 1613, just seven years after the first European colony in North America. The English, however, got word of the colony and attacked it, marking the beginning of a conflict between English and French, one that would continue for more than 150 years as each sought to control this new land.

Paddling northward and looking east toward Smallidge Point, you will see several houses in the town of Northeast Harbor. The only locally owned shorefront property is a piece with a large working wharf extending out into the water; the rest is owned by seasonal residents. As you enter the mouth of Somes Sound, note the tidal current. It always amazes me to sit in my boat and be carried along only by the tide. Look at the water's surface; the occurrence and shape of the waves can be indicators of changes in the bottom topography.

(See "Geology," p. 95.) Flying Mountain rises to the west. Its name comes from the Abenaki, who believed that it was part of St. Sauveur Mountain until it "flew" off. Here the shoreline becomes Cadillac Mountain granite, which continues for the rest of the paddle trip. Rounding Flying Mountain, you come to Valley Cove, one of the most beautiful coves on Mount Desert Island. The tall cliff to the west is St. Sauveur Mountain, named after the colony at Fernald Point. In the 1930s and '40s, peregrine falcons nested here.

The beach in Valley Cove is an ideal place to stop. You can easily see how protected and camouflaged Valley Cove is from the mouth of Somes Sound. Many ships during the French and Indian War staged here while scouts were sent up Flying Mountain to watch the area for incoming ships; surprise attacks were easy and commonplace. I suggest taking your lunch and hiking up Flying Mountain. Follow the trail to the left from the stairs at the back of the beach. It takes about twenty minutes to reach the peak. The view encompasses all of the nearby harbors and the Cranberry Isles.

Continuing up the sound from Valley Cove on the western shoreline, you come to Man o' War Brook. This stream flows down from Acadia Mountain, the third and final peak that shelters Valley Cove. The

Man o' War Brook.
W. DAVID ANDREWS II.

brook cascades over the granite shore in a series of small waterfalls before splashing into the sound. It was easy for a ship to replenish its water supply here while moored in the deep water—hence the brook's name—and just as easy for you and me to paddle up under the falls and bask in the spray.

At the base of Acadia Mountain, on the shore a few hundred yards to the east of Man o' War Brook, is a bronze plaque embedded in the granite. The beautiful monument reads:

> ACADIA MOUNTAIN GIVEN TO THE PUBLIC
> IN MEMORY OF
> REV. CORNELIUS SMITH AND HIS WIFE MARY WHEELER
> WHO WERE PIONEERS OF THE SUMMER COLONY
> AT NORTHEAST HARBOR 1886–1913

Who were these people, and why was a plaque placed at the water's edge for only seafarers to find? I have not found the answers to these quesions, adding to the mystery and romance of the place.

From here, you may choose to continue northward up the sound or cross to the east side of the sound to explore that shore on the return trip. Either way, remember to use caution leaving The Narrows, and watch for boat traffic while returning to your original put-in site.

Upper Somes Sound

DIFFICULTY LEVEL

Intermediate.

AVERAGE TRIP LENGTH

6 nautical miles.

PADDLE SUMMARY

Upper Somes Sound is a beautiful and ecologically intriguing area. You can explore Sargent Cove, a shallow inlet, and Somes Harbor, which is a mudflat at lower tides. There are unbroken views of Somes Sound, a natural fjord, and on the western shore, the historic town and quarry of Hall Quarry.

ITEMS OF INTEREST

HISTORY—Somesville, the first permanent European settlement on Mount Desert Island; Hall Quarry, a well-known quarry and colorful town.

GEOLOGY—Somes Sound is the only natural fjord in the eastern United States.

ECOLOGY—At the head of the sound is an unusual marsh-mudflat ecosystem highly rich in organic matter and supporting ample wildlife, including seals and eagles, great blue herons, and many other birds.

CONDITIONS

The optimal weather for this trip is light to moderate winds (0–15 knots). The head of Somes Sound is fairly protected except in due-north or due-south winds, which become quite strong as they are funneled through the sound. Remember that most of this trip is unprotected, and one leg will be into a headwind. The tides should also be considered: although the channel remains open, allowing you to exit and enter the harbor, some of the area within Somes Harbor becomes a mudflat.

ACCESS

SARGENT DRIVE PICNIC AREA—Turn off Rte. 198 onto Sargent Drive 1.2 miles south of the intersection of Rtes. 198 and 233. After 0.8 mile there is a forked road off to the right, which leads to the picnic area.

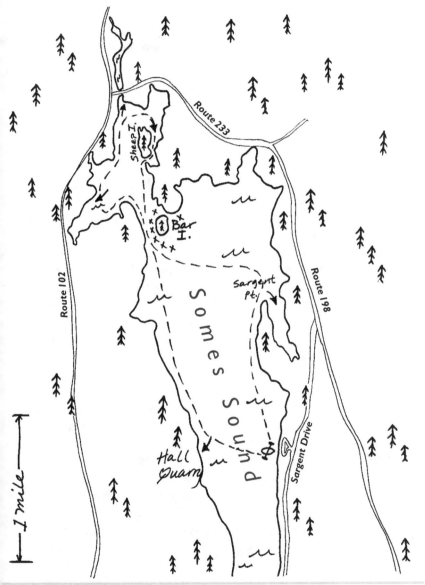

ISLAND OWNERSHIP

BAR ISLAND—Acadia National Park.

SHEEP ISLAND—Maine Bureau of Public Lands.

LANDING SITES

There are no landing sites in this area.

CAUTION AREAS

There are no caution areas in this region.

THE PADDLE

(See "Geology," p. 95.) From the put-in site, follow the eastern shore northward up Somes Sound toward Sargent Point. The shoreline here is Somesville granite, a fine-grained variety, as is the entire shoreline of the trip. Within one mile, you will reach Sargent Point and the entrance to Sargent Cove.

I had paddled Somes Sound several times before I discovered this cove, although my enlightenment came not from a chart, as one might expect. I was on top of Sargent Mountain with some paddling friends, looking at the sound and talking about our paddling adventures. The cove's light green color caught my eye. This unknown area was still on my mind when several of us decided to go exploring a few days later. We found the cove, which has a soft clay/sand bottom, giving it its lighter color.

Leaving the cove, continue northward toward Bar Island. Once owned by descendants of Abraham Somes, the island became part of Acadia National Park in the 1920s. As you approach the entrance to Somes Harbor, pass Bar Island to the west through the main channel.

(See "Environmental Kayaking," p. 146) This island is bald eagle territory, so paddle straight through the channel. Do not stop within one-fourth of a mile of the island (until you are approximately in the middle of the harbor). Your cooperation reduces the amount of disturbance exerted upon these threatened eagles; the pair that live in this area have already moved their nest once, probably due to disturbance.

(See "Social History," p. 135.) Once in the harbor, take a moment to imagine what Abraham Somes and Eden Sutton saw when they first entered this area in 1759. They had been given a land grant by the Mass-

achusetts Bay Colony (at this time Maine was part of Massachusetts) to establish a permanent settlement in the area. Somes and Sutton sailed up the sound seeking land suitable for supporting their families, who would soon follow. They first landed on a great field, the one you see now, finding only portage trails made by Native Americans. Somesville eventually became the first permanent European settlement on the island.

The ecology of this protected harbor at the head of the fjord is unlike any other around Mount Desert Island. The mudflat is surrounded by granite ledge topped with spruce and fir trees, and a river adds fresh water, increasing the area's ecological productivity. The water is warmer and the salinity level is lower than in the rest of Mount Desert's coastal waters. Great blue herons, osprey, eagles, cormorants, loons, and harbor seals are attracted to this ecologically rich environment.

On the east side of the harbor is Sheep Island, which is now owned by the Maine Bureau of Public Lands. Like Bar Island, it was once the property of the Somes family. During the 1850s, there was a boardinghouse on the island. The campground you see is Mount Desert Island Campground, a great place to stay, particularly for boaters, as this facility has its own boat ramp. Exploring the area can be fun, as you have the sense that you are on a lake rather than the ocean.

(See "Geology," p. 95.) Due north within the harbor, a river empties into the sound. On the right as you enter the river inlet, there is a beautiful glacial erratic. This inlet becomes rapids during most of the tidal change (both incoming and outgoing). They can be fun to play in with either a sea kayak or river kayak.

Once you have finished exploring, head southward out of Somes Harbor, again using discretion and caution when passing Bar Island. Continue south

Storm clouds gather overhead as the author paddles by a large erratic in Somes Harbor.
W. DAVID ANDREWS II.

along the western shore of the sound for approximately one mile past Bar Island.

(See "Social History," p. 135.) You will come to the town of Hall Quarry, distinguishable by a boat yard and cut hillside. This is the home of what was one of the most productive and lucrative quarries on the Maine coast. It was begun in 1870 by Cyrus James Hall, who managed the business for the next thirty years. The quarry grew quickly compared to others because of its easy deepwater access, exceptional rock quality, and Hall's foresight.

As the enterprise began to employ more and more workers during the 1880s and '90s, a town grew around it. At its height, the town had several stores, a blacksmith shop, dormitories for unwed workers, and a small theater. The majority of its residents were immigrants from Sweden, Italy, Finland, and Scotland. The superior pink and white granite was used in the Library of Congress in Washington, D.C.; the United States Mint in Philadelphia; and the Philadelphia Customs House and Courthouse.

In 1901, Hall lost an important bid and there was a strike at the quarry. The quarry closed and Hall died six years later, at the age of 73. In 1903, however, the Arthur McMullen Construction Company of New York leased the property and began to once again quarry the rock. During this time the town was officially known as Hall, later to become Hall Quarry. The quarry was subsequently used by various companies; the last rock was cut in the 1950s.

From Hall Quarry, you can return to the Sargent Drive picnic area by heading directly east across the sound.

Geology

*...As the waves rise and fall in broken rhythm on
the shore, as the tide flows and ebbs across the littoral
belt, so the seas of former times have risen
and fallen in uneven measure on the uneasy land;
the rocks have grown and wasted;
the ice of the North has crept down and
melted away—all shifting back and forth in their
cycles of change. Only one scene lies before us
of the many that have floated through the past.*

WILLIAM MORRIS DAVIS

In all of Maine, Mount Desert Island is one of the best places to study geology, and what better way than from a kayak? The study of geology enables us to understand the physical beauty around us, the effect of the environment on our paddling logistics, and the ways that our surroundings direct our interaction with the land.

One reason why Mount Desert Island is such a wonderful geology classroom is that, as in much of Maine (and particularly the islands), the bedrock is often exposed because the soil was scraped away by glaciers during the last ice age. Mount Desert Island has textbook examples of glacial geology, including glacial scratches, U-shaped valleys, a fjord, and *roches moutonnées*. In addition, all three rock types—igneous (created from magma or liquid rock), metamorphic (changed or recrystallized due to heat or pressure), and sedimentary (formed from layered material such as clay or mud)—can be found in the bedrock. Ongoing geologic forces, such as waves and ice, erode and shape the landscape, creating dramatic and intricate cliffs, caves, and arches.

A basic knowledge of geologic formations and processes is important for understanding the appearance of the land today. This discussion of geology begins with a brief analogy of geologic time and then moves on to the most easily seen and apparent geologic formations: the recent effects of erosion. After discussing how to "see" geology, we move back to the time of the glaciers. Finally, we travel even further back, not only in time but abstraction, to the initial creation of Mount Desert Island's bedrocks. Bedrock is the fabric; glaciation creates the texture. What we observe is a garment further trimmed by current geologic forces.

GEOLOGIC TIME

To illustrate the concept of Mount Desert Island's geologic past, I'll start with an analogy to kayaking. The factors that influence what we see around Mount Desert Island today will occur in a ten-hour paddling day.

As you step into your boat at 8 a.m., the time is 500 million years ago and the scenery is very different. It is hot. You're wearing long pants, a long-sleeved shirt, and a large hat; the chance of sunburn is great. All you see is one huge ocean with volcanoes erupting hot lava and ash.

During the first two hours of your trip through this area, which smells of molten rock, steam, and sulfur, the highly layered bedrock Ellsworth schist forms from the settling ash and debris. By lunchtime, the bedrock Bar Harbor formation, layered by the sediments on the bottom of the ocean, and the Cranberry Island series, a cementlike collage of volcanic material, are formed.

During lunch, some of the bedrock is folded and altered by the heat and pressure of the changing environment. The air begins to cool; by the time you have finished eating, it has become very cold. You bring out your extra layers as it begins to snow; an ice age has begun. Throughout the afternoon, the water level continually fluctuates. You negotiate huge waves and currents as climate fluctuations cause the sea to alternately freeze and melt.

As the boating conditions worsen and the day nears its end, you and your party decide to head in. The water level now drops by hun-

GEOLOGIC TIMELINE FEATURING MAJOR EVENTS

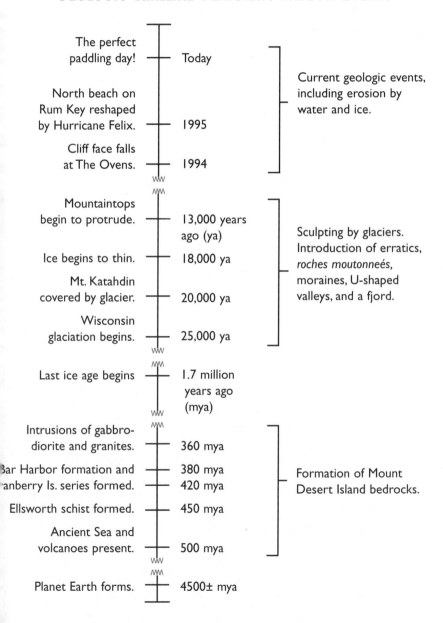

The perfect paddling day! — Today

North beach on Rum Key reshaped by Hurricane Felix. — 1995

Cliff face falls at The Ovens. — 1994

Current geologic events, including erosion by water and ice.

Mountaintops begin to protrude. — 13,000 years ago (ya)

Ice begins to thin. — 18,000 ya

Mt. Katahdin covered by glacier. — 20,000 ya

Wisconsin glaciation begins. — 25,000 ya

Sculpting by glaciers. Introduction of erratics, *roches moutonneés,* moraines, U-shaped valleys, and a fjord.

Last ice age begins — 1.7 million years ago (mya)

Intrusions of gabbro-diorite and granites. — 360 mya

Bar Harbor formation and Cranberry Is. series formed. — 380 mya — 420 mya

Ellsworth schist formed. — 450 mya

Ancient Sea and volcanoes present. — 500 mya

Formation of Mount Desert Island bedrocks.

Planet Earth forms. — 4500± mya

dreds of feet at a time, and you can see a glacier approaching in the distance. Before you are able to comprehend your situation, you find yourself and your boat on an ice sheet; the glacier has arrived. As you turn your head to look, the ice sheet melts and sea level rises again dramatically.

As you thankfully near your takeout site, a tip of land becomes visible. The re-emerging land gradually rebounds once the weight of the glacier has been removed. The land has been drastically reshaped, carved by the ice sheet that flowed across it. As you approach only feet from shore, beaches form, cliffs become steeper, and animal life erupts around you. A Viking ship appears in the background as your bow touches shore. Now safe on land, you look back over your shoulder, only to see a whale-watch boat whiz past.

CURRENT GEOLOGICAL FORCES

Many forces mold the geologic character of Mount Desert Island's surface. The two most active—waves and ice—create beaches, sandbars, cliffs, and sea caves. These easily seen geologic formations play a very active role in almost any kayak trip.

BEACHES: In more than 2,500 miles of shoreline along the Maine coast, fewer than 60 miles are sandy beaches, and most of these occur in the southern part of the state. Around Mount Desert Island, there is little sand; in fact, the largest beach, Sand Beach, is not crushed rock but primarily crushed shells (from 40 to 85 percent), which is why the flat grains stick to your skin. This is similar to the beaches along the east coast of Florida, which are also made up of calcium carbonate from crushed shells. The only true sand beach on Mount Desert Island is Seal Harbor; it is a wonderful place to launch a kayak, with access to the Cranberry Islands and Somes Sound.

The majority of beaches on Mount Desert Island are cobblestone. Paddling around virtually any bend in the shoreline can lead to a small pocket of beautifully colored rocks pounded smooth and sculpted by the sea—like a giant nursery of dinosaur eggs. In the late 1700s, the wave-tumbled cobblestones, locally called "popplestones," were sold to coastal trading ships as ballast. During the nineteenth century these stones were used to pave the streets of East Coast cities.

A popplestone beach known as Monument Cove.
W. DAVID ANDREWS II.

During hurricane Felix, in the summer of 1995, the entire cobble beach on Rum Key in Frenchman Bay was shifted over the course of four days. The movement of several tons of these baseball-sized rocks uncovered some rock ledge while burying other previously exposed ledge. The entire shape of the beach was altered.

While paddling around Mount Desert Island, take a moment to closely examine the cobble beaches. What are the types of rock? Are the stones uniformly distributed or are they separated by size? What is the general shape of the rocks? And what has caused these patterns? These questions provide a structure from which to seek answers and start a journey of understanding. As we observe how every tide re-shapes the beach, we begin to understand that geology is as much a science of the present as of the past.

SANDBARS: An accumulation of sand and crushed rock often creates sandbars. In sheltered environments, often between land masses, the sand is deposited and shaped by currents and waves. There are several sandbars around Mount Desert Island that are exposed at low tide, including the Bar Harbor Bar, The Hop, and Moose Island. The best indication of the frequency of sandbars, however, is the number of "Bar Islands" along the Maine coast.

CLIFFS: Although originally created by glaciers, the tall, steep cliffs for which Mount Desert Island is famous are also shaped by water and ice. Water seeps into cracks and joints in the rock, expands when frozen, and plucks away slabs and boulders. These cliffs can be seen by paddlers at The Ovens, the Porcupines, and Ironbound Island in Frenchman Bay.

Sometime between late summer 1993 and early summer 1994, a cliff face fell near The Ovens in Upper Frenchman Bay. Although this might seem like a small occurrence to some, the day I saw the remains of that cliff face, now a pile of Bar Harbor formation being washed by waves, I had a greater comprehension of geologic time and significance. We often tend to think of geological changes as occurring over great spans of time, but in fact some can manifest themselves suddenly and dramatically.

SEA CAVES, ARCHES, AND KEYHOLES: Many islands are dotted with nature's sculptures, and a keen eye is all that is needed to find them. Sea caves, arches, and keyholes—also created by the plucking action of ice and erosion of waves—are dependent upon bedrock types. They occur most often in Bar Harbor formation, where the layers are easily broken and separated due to the joints or fractures pre-existing in this bedrock. Water either enters these cracks or erodes dikes of softer rock. There are several places to see these formations, including The Ovens and on Burnt Porcupine, along the Shore Route, and on Long Porcupine, Ironbound, and Sutton

An arch on Long Porcupine Island.
W. DAVID ANDREWS II.

Islands. These locations all have Bar Harbor formation shorelines.

SHORELINE TYPES: The three types of shoreline existing around Mount Desert Island serve as general indications of the three bedrock types found here. These differing shorelines affect the kayaker more than any other geologic feature.

A shoreline made of a relatively weak rock, such as Bar Harbor formation, is rugged, with sharp corners and edges and occasional long, flat slabs. This shoreline is easily eroded, leading to the formation of cliffs and caves. The shore of the town of Bar Harbor is an excellent place to examine this type of coast.

A shoreline made of hard rock, usually granite, erodes much more slowly; waves and ice have little effect. There are relatively few beaches on a granite shoreline and almost no landing places for a boat. The only place on Mount Desert Island with this type of shoreline exclusively is Somes Sound. (This is not a good place to be if you have to relieve yourself. I remember being acutely aware of the lack of landing sites one time when I was paddling along the western shore of the sound. I subsequently devised another use for my bailer.)

The third type of shoreline occurs at a contact, or shatter, zone where different bedrocks, consisting of both hard and soft rock, meet and create a mixed shoreline. Northeast Harbor and Moose Island are two locations to see this type.

THE GLACIERS

One of the greatest contributors to the present appearance of Mount Desert Island was the most recent ice age. The carving and sculpting of the glacial ice can be seen in the beautiful alternating mountains and valleys that give Mount Desert Island its dramatic profile.

THE ICE AGES: The most recent glaciers began to form over most of Canada and the northern United States 1.7 million years ago. These giant flows of ice grew as more snow fell in winter than melted during the summer. Several phases occurred during this ice age; geologists differ on exactly how many times the ice sheet advanced and retreated across the continent. We can see evidence only of the last period, the Wisconsin glacier, because each phase obliterates the effects of the previous glacier.

The Wisconsin period began approximately 25,000 years ago as the ice began to advance toward New England. By about 20,000 years ago, the ice was at least one mile thick over Maine, for we know that it covered Mount Katahdin in Baxter State Park. It extended south to Long Island and southeast approximately 350 to 400 miles into the Gulf of Maine. Then, beginning 18,000 years ago, the ice began to thin; 13,000 years ago, the highest mountaintops saw the light of day. During the Wisconsin period, glaciers covered Mount Desert Island for at least 10,000 years.

CHANGES IN THE LANDSCAPE: Glaciers affected the landscape in many ways. One factor was the great weight of the ice. One square inch of ice one mile thick weighs more than a ton; an acre of ice one mile thick weighs 7 million tons; one cubic mile of ice weighs 4.5 billion tons. This weight caused the land beneath to sink at a ratio of 3:1; beneath the one-mile-thick ice, Maine's land sank one-third of a mile. As the ice thinned and melted, however, the land began to rise, or rebound, accelerating erosion.

Another effect of glaciation was the change in sea level. Imagine Frenchman Bay if so much of the Earth's water was frozen into glaciers that sea level dropped 200 to 300 feet below where it is today. Most of what is now paddling territory would be land. Mount Desert Island would be a peninsula off of the mainland and Bald Porcupine would be a mountaintop. Later, when the glaciers melted faster than the land could rebound, sea level, at its highest point, rose to approximately 250 feet above its current position. This high level is called the upper marine limit. Bar Harbor was underwater, and Mount Desert Island was a much smaller island, farther out to sea. Sea caves and arches formed during this time can be seen on mountainsides in Acadia National Park.

Glaciers also altered the surface geology. When ice travels over land, glacial till (gravel and rocks) collects within the ice. This accumulation acts like sandpaper, scraping the earth and creating scratches, or striations, which are seen on several of the mountains in this area. This abrasion lowered the elevation of the land by three to six feet. As the glacier scraped, it also removed soil, accounting for the relatively thin soil of the coast and islands—a factor that strongly influenced the lives of early island settlers and still affects coastal Mainers today.

U-SHAPED VALLEYS: The many U-shaped valleys on Mount Desert Island were also formed by glaciers. As the ice advanced, it briefly stopped at what was then a solid ridge of mountains running east-west, with only a few streams flowing to the north or south from the top of the range. As the ice and pressure built up, the glacier eventually broke through, and long fingers of ice extended out, modifying the small riverbeds into steep-sided valleys with flat floors. These alternating hills and valleys are easily seen, particularly on the south side of Mount Desert Island, from the Cranberry Isles. Most of the lakes on the island occupy these valleys. So does Somes Sound—this valley merges into the ocean and is called a fjord.

ROCHE MOUTONNÉE: Another glacially formed feature seen around Mount Desert Island is known as a *roche moutonnée,* meaning "sheep rock." Another name for this formation is whaleback. Both terms are clear descriptions of these rock formations, which have a gradual incline on the one side and steep cliffs on the other side. Imagine a round lump of clay (the mountain) and your hand (the glacier). If you were to press down gently on the clay, push your hand forward, and then withdraw it, the clay would be gently sloping on one side and steep on the other. As the southward-moving glacier

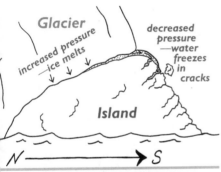

Glacial forces create the roche moutonnée *shape of the Porcupine Islands and Mount Desert.*

pushed on the north side of the mountains, pressure increased and the bottom of the ice melted. This water then seeped into all the cracks and fractures on the south side. As the pressure was released, the water froze, expanded and plucked away the south side of the mountains to make an even steeper cliff. Not only is the entire island of Mount Desert a *roche moutonnée,* but the Porcupine Islands in Frenchman Bay are all textbook-perfect examples.

GLACIAL ERRATIC: Stray boulders, called glacial erratics, are picked up, carried by the ice, and deposited elsewhere. Although most are usually carried only a few miles from their original home, some erratics have been carried up to 100 miles. Erratics can be found all over Mount

A glacial erratic known as Balance Rock is located near the Shore Path on Mount Desert Island.
W. David Andrews II.

Desert Island and the surrounding islands, specifically along the Shore Route, on Bar and Bartlett Islands, and at the head of Somes Sound.

MORAINE: As the period of glaciation drew to a close approximately 10,000 years ago, the receding ice sheet once again modified the landscape. When the glacier melted, it left a ridge of rock debris, called a terminal moraine, that it had scraped and plowed several hundred miles out into the Gulf of Maine. Named Georges Bank, this deposit helps to create the estuary-like ecology of the gulf. Because the bank reduces the flushing of the gulf waters into the rest of the Atlantic and traps the influx of fresh water from the land, this relatively shallow area became one of the richest fishing areas in the world. These fishing grounds were what eventually led to the early exploration and settlement of the Maine coast. Today, however, we realize that the oceans are not an endless resource; the abundance and diversity of species in the gulf fishing industry have been severely depleted.

MOUNT DESERT ISLAND'S BEDROCK FORMATION

Long before the ice ages, the bedrock of Mount Desert Island was created by an ancient sea that covered Maine and the rest of New England more than 500 million years ago. This was also a volcanically active area at that time. Three bedrocks were created: Ellsworth schist, Bar Harbor formation, and Cranberry Island series. All three rock types, vastly different in nature and appearance, can be seen in many locations as you paddle in the Mount Desert Island area.

ELLSWORTH SCHIST: Sand, silt, mud, and volcanic ash settled in thin layers at the bottom of the sea to form the first bedrock. Once settled, these layers then metamorphosed, changing with heat and pressure from the surrounding environment, to form schist, a metamorphic rock similar to slate, the material that blackboards were once made of. The schist then folded and bent, changing from even, flat, horizontal layers to jumbled and twisted layers.

This beautiful light gray rock, braided with quartz and feldspar veins, looks like marble cake and is one of my favorite rocks. It can be seen

Ellsworth schist. Note the marbleized appearance.
W. DAVID ANDREWS II.

at Thompson Island and Hadley Point in the Mount Desert Narrows, on the west side of Bartlett Island, and on the shoreline of Seal Cove.

BAR HARBOR FORMATION: This sedimentary rock was also formed from the layers of sand and gravel deposited by the ocean 420 million years ago. The layering in this rock is highly organized and consists of siltstone and sandstone. The rock layers appear gray, red, and brown and are easily eroded, creating caves,

The sedimentary Bar Harbor formation is a prominent rock type along the shores of Bar Harbor.
W. DAVID ANDREWS II.

keyholes, arches, and cliffs. Examples can be seen along the Shore Route, on the Porcupines, at The Ovens, on Ironbound and Bear Islands, and at the entrance to Northeast Harbor.

CRANBERRY ISLAND SERIES: This igneous rock was formed by the cooling and crystallization of magma, or liquid rock, and ash from ancient volcanoes 450 million years ago. The Cranberry Island series is a fine, light-gray ash rock with irregular fragments. Good examples are hard to

Cranberry Island series. The mussel shell is to the right of a chunk of volcanic material within the host rock.
W. DAVID ANDREWS II.

find, but you can look for it on Little and Great Cranberry Islands, on Sutton and Greening Islands, and along the shoreline of Southwest Harbor.

MAGMA INVASIONS

GABBRO-DIORITE: After the formation of bedrock, two invasions of magma, or molten rock, began 360 to 380 million years ago. The first invasion, occurring on the west side of Mount Desert Island, consisted of gabbro (a dark gray rock) and diorite (a lighter gray rock). These two rocks are very similar in appearance and are often intermixed; both

Gabbro-diorite.
W. DAVID ANDREWS II.

types are heavily jointed and jagged. Veins of quartz are common, in addition to rusty iron sulfide, sometimes giving the rock a brown appearance. An excellent place to see gabbro-diorite is along the northern shore of all the Porcupine Islands. It can also be seen on Thomas Island and The Twinnies, and along the Thomas Bay shoreline in the Mount Desert Narrows. Hardwood Island and the Pretty Marsh Harbor shoreline on the west side of the Mount Desert Island are also good locations.

GRANITES: The second invasion, mostly on the east side of Mount Desert Island, is granite, the most commonly found rock type on the island. A brewing pot of molten rock began to form under the island, flowing upward into zones of weakness, joints and fractures between layers of bedrock, and around the edges of the bedrock. Not only were new rock types introduced, but the roof of the existing bedrock collapsed and sank as the magma gushed up and over the top and sides, resulting in what is now a central granite mass surrounded by a shatter, or contact, zone of older rocks. This contact zone can be seen on Moose Island and in Northeast Harbor.

Granite is an intrusive igneous rock (meaning that the magma cooled within the earth) made up of several minerals that cooled and crystallized at different rates, including quartz (a glassy mineral), feldspar (pink or gray), hornblende (black), and biotite (also black but in thin layers, or plates). The difference between gray and pink granite lies in the feldspar. If the feldspar has inclusions of the mineral magnetite, it is black, creating gray granite. If it is rich in hematite mineral inclusions, it is red, creating pink granite. The different grain sizes of the rocks are caused by different cooling rates of the magma. If a rock cools slowly, the crystals are large; if a rock cools quickly, the crystals are small.

The first granite to invade was finely grained. Located close to the surface, it cooled very quickly and thus has small crystals. It is light gray with a tan and pink hue. Known as Southwest Harbor granite, it is found along the shoreline in Southwest Harbor, and on Greening and Sutton Islands.

Coarse-grained granite soon followed. Found on the eastern half of Mount Desert Island, it is called Cadillac Mountain granite. Its bumpy texture is due to the slow cooling and subsequent large crystals in the rock. Finally, medium-grained granite invaded the west and central part of Mount Desert Island. Known as Somesville granite, it is pink and gray and looks much like Cadillac Mountain granite except that the crystals are slightly smaller. It makes up the entire shoreline of Upper Somes Sound and was heavily quarried during the 1800s and early to mid-1900s.

DIKES AND VEINS: The last change that occurred during the intrusion of magma was the introduction of dikes and veins. Dikes are formed when hot magma, or igneous rock, flows into an open fracture in solid rock. Many dikes on Mount Desert Island are either basalt or diabase, both fine-grained intrusive igneous rocks that are usually

This example of a basaltic dike within granite bedrock is approximately two feet wide and extends for more than forty feet.
W. DAVID ANDREWS II.

blackish-gray. The edges, or walls, are smooth and parallel; they can be up to 100 feet long and several feet wide. Because of the different cooling rates of the exterior and interior of the dike, it is fine grained on the outer edge and has larger crystals in the middle. Veins are much smaller than dikes and run parallel to each other or appear as braided ribbons of minerals within the host rock. Many of the veins on the island are quartz. Both dikes and veins can be seen throughout the greater Mount Desert area.

Marine Ecology

Read Nature not in books. If you study Nature in books,
when you go out-of-doors you cannot find her.
LOUIS AGASSIZ

The coast and Gulf of Maine are productive environments that have been studied for many years. The famous naturalists John James Audubon and Louis Agassiz were fascinated by the diversity of the area and studied Mount Desert Island in particular. An 1877 visitors' guide to Mount Desert Island colorfully describes this wonderful variety:

> . . . bleak mountain-sides and sunny nook in sheltered cove; frowning precipice and gentle, smiling meadow; broad, heaving ocean and placid mountain lake; dashing sea-foam and glistening trout brook; the deep thunder of the ground swell, and the solemn stillness of the mountain gorge; the impetuous rush and splash of surf and the musical cadence of far-off waterfalls, all mingle and blend in the memory of this wonderful land.[1]

Mount Desert Island lies on the boundary of two ornithological and botanical zones. To the south, the environment is influenced by the Gulf Stream, which produces warm summer and fall seasons. To the north, the environment is influenced by the boreal (Northern Temperate and Subarctic) region; the result is cold offshore waters, rich in

1. Clara Barnes Martin, *Loring, Short, and Harmon's Illustrated Guide Book for Mount Desert Island.* 4th edition (Portland, Maine, 1877), p. 26.

wildlife. Mount Desert Island is not only the home to organisms from both environments, but is also located on a major bird migratory route.

This chapter discusses the uniqueness of the Gulf of Maine and island ecology, the intertidal zones and marine organisms, birds, and sea mammals. I invite you to explore the wonders of the oceanic world and the interrelationship between humans and their environment that has been so prominent and vital along the Maine coast.

GULF OF MAINE

To understand the great variety and richness of marine life that await the kayaker in the Mount Desert Island area, it is important to first look at the heart of this ecosystem, the Gulf of Maine. This young sea, only 15,000 years old, covers 36,000 square miles and averages only 200 feet deep. Five major rivers—the Merrimack, Piscataqua, Kennebec, Penobscot, and St. John—flow into the gulf. They deliver large amounts of nutrients and lower the overall salinity level. In effect, this creates a huge estuary, one of the most biologically productive ecosystems in the world. It also creates an ecotone, the boundary between two ecosystems, that is more productive than each alone. The gulf is cold and thus able to hold greater amounts of carbon dioxide and oxygen, the two most needed elements for life.

This large influx of fresh water, the confluence of two major currents (the Gulf Stream and the Labrador Current), and large tides within the gulf all help create upwelling, overturns, and continual mixing throughout the entire water column, a process that sustains this rich environment. The dark green water characteristic of the gulf is evidence of its abundant plant and animal life. It is this dark water that I love, for it adds to the mystery and wonder of the world that lies below my boat.

(See "Social History," p. 135.) The productive fishing grounds that resulted from this rich environment eventually led to the settlement of the coastal lands surrounding the Gulf of Maine. Today, this vital natural region, which significantly influences the climate and ecology of New England and the Maritime Provinces—not to mention many human activities, from fishing to commerce to recreation—is an ecosystem in crisis. Overfishing and pollution have led to the decline of its biodiversity.

ISLAND ECOLOGY

Islands are fragile and isolated ecosystems. They are often small parcels of land, limited in their renewable resources such as plant seeds and young animals. Island living is stressful because environmental conditions are extremely variable due to wind, waves, salt, and human impact—even more so than on the mainland. Single events, such as fire or the introduction of a foreign predator, can be devastating.

During the 1800s, islands were heavily settled; forests were cleared, fields were cut, and nonnative animals and plants were introduced. Although most islands have had few residents since the turn of the twentieth century (except those that have been used for sheep grazing) and have begun to return to their wild state, their original ecosystems have not returned. Instead of the original mixed-hardwoods forest, island trees today are predominantly spruce and fir. Hardwood Island in Blue Hill Bay and Ironbound Island in Frenchman Bay, are among the few islands in the Mount Desert area that still have patches of the original species such as oak, beech, birch, and maple.

As more and more boaters begin to visit these islands, it is important to keep in mind their particularly fragile and limited environment. Our influence as kayakers is significant and our actions are critical. A later chapter, "Environmental Kayaking," explains our particular impact as paddlers and outlines minimum-impact behavior both on the water and on the islands.

INTERTIDAL ZONES

At the edge of the sea, two worlds, the terrestrial and the aquatic, meet and mingle. This creates what is called an edge effect (like that of fresh and salt water mixing in the Gulf of Maine), an ecotone with a greater abundance and variety of species than either of its two parts. This dynamic shoreline and its inhabitants must constantly change in response to climatic and geological events occurring both on a grand scale, such as the freezing and melting of glaciers, and on a local scale, such as human influence, storms, and tides.

In the intertidal zones, organisms must adapt to extreme environmental factors, creating a unique world of oddities and specialization. With great fluctuation in surrounding water and air, and variations in temperature, salinity, and physical pressure, intertidal organisms are highly adapted to their particular environment.

Wherever you paddle, upon close examination you will be able to see the patterns and beauty of the intertidal zones. This might be as subtle as a worn limpet spot on a rock or as dramatic as the abrupt line between the white barnacle zone and the black/spray zone.

The predominant factor influencing intertidal life is, not surprisingly, the tide, which affects all organisms—how they feed, their body shape, how and when they reproduce, their method of protection, and even their color. Most important, the tide influences where an organism lives within the intertidal zone—the simplest form of adaptation. These intertidal zones subsequently become a horizontally layered environment, regarded as one of the clearest examples of zonation in the natural world. The shoreline is nature's canvas; zonation is her finished work.

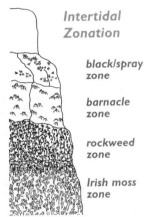

Intertidal Zonation

black/spray zone

barnacle zone

rockweed zone

Irish moss zone

BLACK/SPRAY ZONE: Looking at a rock face, say the southeastern shore of Bartlett Island (a particularly wonderful place to study the intertidal zones), you'll notice that the top is bare; neither terrestrial vegetation nor sea creatures live here. The next area down is the black, or spray, zone, which supports either blue-green algae (*Calothrix*) or a black lichen (*Verrucaria*). The blue-green algae is very slippery; the lichen looks like thin black pavement or black spots. Although preferring air, they can withstand both saltwater spray and freshwater from runoff.

BARNACLE ZONE: The next layer, in sharp contrast, is the barnacle zone. Its bright white color makes it easy to identify. This zone begins at the high-tide mark and must withstand regular submersion and powerful physical pressure from waves and surf. The barnacle, a crustacean, is highly specialized to tolerate this physical stress.

ROCKWEED ZONE: The next zone appears as brown hair or fur covering the rocks. This is the rockweed zone, whose inhabitants spend almost equal time in and out of the water. The predominant types of rockweed are bladder wrack (*Fucus*) occurring in the upper level, and

Knotted Wrack

knotted wrack *(Ascophyllum)* occurring in the lower level. Bladder rockweed is a flat, thin brown seaweed with a raised midrib and air bladders only at the tips of the fronds. Knotted wrack has longer, rounded, fingerlike fronds with no midrib; the air bladders occur along the length of the fronds. With small air bladders to keep them afloat when submerged, these two seaweeds photosynthesize. They have strong flesh to withstand the force of crashing waves. Both algae are very slippery, so be care-

Bladder Wrack

ful when getting out of your boat. Many other intertidal organisms are also found in this zone.

IRISH MOSS ZONE: The next zone toward the water is also inhabited predominantly by seaweed, though it is slightly redder in appearance and grows only a few inches long. This zone, consisting mostly of Irish moss

(Chondrus crispus), occurs just above the low-tide line. This seaweed can stand only limited exposure to air. A short-branched red seaweed, Irish moss was traditionally used as a thickener for blancmange, a dessert. In Maine, it was once heavily harvested for manufacture of carrageenan, a food additive used in many products, such as toothpaste, hand creams, diet foods, chocolate milk, puddings, and ice cream.

KELP ZONE: The zone at or below the low-tide mark is the kelp zone, dominated by a large, leathery brown seaweed *(Laminaria agardhii)* with a single long, ruffled, flat blade without a midrib, looking like a huge lasagna noodle. This zone, always underwater, does not have to withstand the harsh waves to which higher zones are subjected. Like its smaller relatives, kelp attaches itself to rocks or mussels by means of a branched holdfast. The anchor usually rips free before the hold-

fast breaks. Kayakers will most commonly find dislodged blades of kelp floating freely on the water's surface. I have occasionally found blades up to twenty feet long, and like to wrap them around me like a huge feathery boa.

INTERTIDAL CREATURES

Within and among the zones of the intertidal world, is an array of many intriguing animals. Here are brief descriptions of the most commonly seen organisms that you will find while kayaking or exploring during your lunch break.

ROCK, OR ACORN, BARNACLE *(BALANUS BALANOIDES)*: The most prominent intertidal organism is the barnacle. Related to the lobster, crab, and shrimp, this highly specialized crustacean was described by nineteenth-century naturalist Louis Agassiz as "nothing more than a little shrimp-

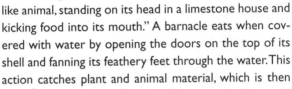

like animal, standing on its head in a limestone house and kicking food into its mouth." A barnacle eats when covered with water by opening the doors on the top of its shell and fanning its feathery feet through the water. This action catches plant and animal material, which is then brought into the shell to the barnacle's mouth. If you watch a barnacle very carefully, you can see this process.

This high-intertidal animal has adapted to its harsh environment most clearly with its conical shape and shell material, which allow it to withstand up to forty pounds per square inch of pressure. The shells of these organisms are razor sharp and will cut your feet if you try to walk barefoot across barnacle-covered ledges. The glue that holds a barnacle to a rock is one of the strongest adhesives known; scientists are trying to duplicate it for use in dentistry. The barnacle can withstand temperatures from 5 to 110 degrees Fahrenheit, a feat that few other marine animals can accomplish.

PERIWINKLE *(LITTORINA)*: Almost as common as barnacles, periwinkles are the marine equivalent of *escargot* and just as tasty. They have a smooth brown shell with a round opening on the underside. This vegetarian aquatic snail can eat both in and out of the water. There are three species of periwinkles, each preferring a different intertidal zone. The smooth periwinkle *(L. obtusata)* lives in the lower tidal zone, the common periwinkle *(L. littorea)* in the mid-tidal zone, and the rough periwinkle *(L. saxatilis)* in the high intertidal zone.

DOG WHELK *(THAIS LAPILLUS)*: Dog whelks are carnivorous snails that forage by either drilling a hole through or prying open the shell of their

prey. Because they feed on the two dominant intertidal organisms, mussels and barnacles, whelks play a critical role in maintaining a population balance in the intertidal community. They come in many colors, including white, yellow, orange, and striped. Their shell is larger than that of a periwinkle and is grooved or rough. The underside opening is oval. In ancient times, whelks were used to make Tyrian purple dye; a secretion from their anal gland turns purple when exposed to sunlight.

LIMPET *(ACMAEA TESTUDINALIS)*: Called Chinaman's hat, the limpet has a conical shell. They travel on their large, fleshy foot to feed, but during

low tide, secure themselves tightly to rocks, trapping water to prevent drying out. Their strong homing instinct brings them back to the same spot between tides, and eventually perfect, limpet-sized depressions become worn into the rock.

STARFISH *(ASTERIAS)*: A starfish has thousands of little tube suction feet that allow it to move among the rocks. Although seemingly gentle, the starfish is strong and forceful; to eat, it wraps its legs around its prey—usually a clam or scallop—pries open the shell, inserts its stomach, and digests the animal on the spot. The starfish leaves only an empty shell to be found later by an inquisitive paddler.

SAND DOLLAR *(ECHINARACHNIUS PARMA)*: Related to the starfish and sea

urchin, though less commonly found, the sand dollar looks like a circular, flat shell. When alive it is covered with fine brown spines that look like short fur; when dead and washed ashore, it turns white and the five "petals" inscribed in the shell reveal its relationship to the starfish, with its five legs. The small spines of the sand dollar aid in feeding and breathing.

GREEN SEA URCHIN *(STRONGYLOCENTROTUS DROBACHIENSIS)*: The green sea urchin (which bears the longest Latin name of any organism), is affectionately viewed as "the weed of the sea." Looking like a slightly flattened baseball, the urchin is cousin to the starfish and is covered with green spines up to half an inch long (which aid in movement). It has an anus opening on top of the shell, and a larger mouth opening on the bottom. Mostly vegetarian, sea urchins have very large appetites and can wipe out entire kelp forests.

There is currently a gold rush in Maine—diving and dragging for sea urchins. While kayaking, you might see divers or boats displaying the international dive flag (a red rectangle with a white diagonal stripe) or draggers towing a long net. Urchin eggs, or roe, are sold to Japan. Some areas are already reporting severe depletion of urchin populations, and overharvesting is beginning to curtail this boom.

BLUE MUSSEL *(MYTILUS EDULIS)*: The common edible blue mussel is a bivalve that attaches itself to the ocean floor, rocks, or another mussel by strong hairlike strands called byssal threads, or byssi. Their beautiful crescent-shaped, shiny blue shells can be found on many beaches. Mussels can colonize an area faster than any other marine organism, including barnacles. Mussels form "pearls" around any foreign object within their tissue, so eating them can be hazardous to the fillings in your teeth. Be sure to check on the presence of red tide before eating any filter-feeders. (The telephone number for red tide information is listed in Appendix A.)

CRABS: If you spend time exploring in the rockweed, you might spot a crab. The most common types of crab are the green crab *(Carcinus maenas)*, the rock crab *(Cancer irroratus)*, and the hermit crab *(Pagurtis acadianus)*.

Green crabs are dark greenish yellow, less than three inches across, and very active. Rock crabs are reddish yellow and grow up to seven inches across. Hermit crabs, although true crabs, have no hard exoskeleton and therefore must borrow one from elsewhere; they can

rock crab

green crab

often be found hiding in old periwinkle shells. They do molt and grow, however, and periodically need to find a new and bigger shell. I was recently told of a hermit crab that had adopted a small plastic toy fire truck as its home.

LOBSTER *(HOMARUS AMERICANUS)*: Dark green with blue and reddish blotches and a light yellowish underbelly, lobsters turn bright red only when they are cooked. Lobsters eat crabs, clams, mussels, starfish, urchins, and other lobsters. In summer, they migrate from offshore to shallower water. A century ago, these crustaceans were so abundant that they could be picked off the rocks by hand at low tide. Eating lobster was a sign of poverty, and prison inmates and indentured servants were legally protected against having to eat lobster more often than two or three times a week.

Today, the average catch is 0.7 pounds per trap (most lobsters you eat weigh one to one and a half pounds), so less than one marketable lobster is caught per trap. The most productive season is late summer and fall, right after the lobsters have molted and the tourists have gone home. Lobstering is the number-one industry on the coast of Maine, and 50 percent of the lobsters harvested in New England are from Maine.

JELLYFISH: Two types of jellyfish inhabit Maine waters. The moon jellyfish *(Aurelia aurita)* is a small, transparent, harmless organism with four small circles on top, hence the name. This jellyfish is very common, and often during the summer there will be population explosions, or large hatches. I once encountered a huge mass of them so thick that they fell off my paddle as I lifted it out of the water.

The lion's mane, or red arctic jellyfish *(Cyanea capillata)* is poisonous and should be avoided. This large jellyfish is red or pink and has long tentacles. While paddling, you'll be safe floating over one, but don't put your hands in the water, swim if they are nearby, or touch one that has washed up on shore. The trailing tentacles, which are sometimes hard to see, will sting, causing a painful, albeit short-lived, welt. While they can grow up to 6 feet in diameter, in Maine waters they are rarely more than  two feet across. (This organism was the mysterious killer in one Sherlock Holmes mystery.)

BIRDS

Mount Desert Island is a special place to watch birds. A great variety and abundance of birds are present because of the many islands and the protection they offer, the amount of food in the Gulf of Maine, and the existence of Acadia National Park, which decreases the amount of island-wide development. Bird species from both the South and the Arctic are present. Of 400 bird species found within the state of Maine, 320 can be seen on Mount Desert Island.

At the turn of the twentieth century, however, the situation was different. Seeing a seabird, for example, was rare. Birds were hunted by coastal fishermen for their eggs, meat, and feathers (for down and fashion). At that time, hunting and fishing practices did not incorporate the concept of long-term sustainability. While coastal fishermen took several hundred years to deplete the fish population, because fish have a high reproductive capacity and fishing was inherently inefficient, the seabird population was severely depleted in only twenty years (between 1880 and 1900), because birds produce only a few young each year and entire colonies could be harvested at one time.

Bird hunters justified the great number taken by reasoning that the Arctic-breeding species occurred in far greater abundance to the north. This was true, but because many of the hunted species *were* at the edge of their breeding range, their depleted populations were unable to recover in Maine.

Many birds were hunted nearly to extinction; one species, the flightless great auk, did in fact become extinct. This bird, belonging to the family that includes puffins, razorbills and guillemots, was the most powerful diving bird ever, able to dive to a depth of 240 feet. Because of its inability to fly, entire colonies could be driven onto shore and clubbed to death. Ironically, the last two birds alive were taken on June 3, 1844, to be stuffed and placed in the Royal University Museum, Copenhagen, Denmark.

Several factors at the turn of the century led to the recovery of the bird populations. Public pressure against the fashion of plumed hats began to increase, which led to the founding of the National Audubon Society, one of the oldest and

The now-extinct great auk was, like the penguin, a superb underwater swimmer.

largest private conservation organizations in the world. Additionally, as the residents of many island communities moved inland, other sources of meat and eggs became available, decreasing the reliance on seabirds. And as more island nesting sites again became available, some islands became bird sanctuaries, eventually protected by such organizations as the Maine Department of Inland Fisheries and Wildlife, the U.S. Fish and Wildlife Service, the National Audubon Society, and the Maine Audubon Society. Finally, the Migratory Bird Treaty Act of 1918 put an end to the hunting. As a result, many birds, almost all of the species you will see around Mount Desert Island, began the slow path to recovery. The following descriptions are a brief introduction to the birds you will mostly likely see while kayaking in the area.

GULLS *(LARUS)*: By far the most common and underrated seabirds are the gulls. They are affectionately known as dump ducks, beach chickens, and, by a dear friend of mine, sky rats. Once close to extinction, they have rebounded more successfully than any other bird species on the coast of Maine, far surpassing their original numbers. Gulls' production of multiple eggs, their aggressive behavior, and their adaptability have all contributed to their quick recovery. Fish-industry waste and the once-common open garbage dumps have also provided a boost for the gulls.

Like most other seabirds, gulls are monogamous, with males and females taking an equal role in raising the young. They have a life span of up to forty years. They typically eat fish, crabs, sea urchins, clams, and kelp. There are three types of gulls around Mount Desert Island: the great black-backed gull, the herring gull, and the laughing gull.

GREAT BLACK-BACKED GULL *(L. MARINUS)*: Black-backed gulls are the largest and most dominant member of the gull community, though not

the most common. Black-backs did not begin to breed on the coast of Maine until 1926, yet they have experienced one of the most rapid population recoveries of any seabird. Their large size and distinctive black wings easily differentiate adult black-backs from other gulls. Black-backs are aggressive, stealing fish from other birds and eating the eggs and young chicks of other gulls, terns, shorebirds, and eider ducks. They have contributed significantly to the decline of the tern.

I remember floating off Long Porcupine in Frenchman Bay and watching a black-back land on the head of a cormorant that had just surfaced with a fish in its mouth. The cormorant protested having its food stolen right out of its mouth but was no match for the gull, which flew away quickly, lunch and all.

HERRING GULL *(L. ARTENTATUS)*: Herring gulls are some of the most common seabirds; you should see at least one, if not ten to a hundred, while paddling. They are slightly smaller than black-backs and have light gray wings. Sexually mature herring gulls have a red dot on their bills; a young gull feeds by pecking the dot, which stimulates the adult to regurgitate food for the chick. Herring gulls are quite intelligent; they have a small vocabulary and complex vocalizations. Recognition among birds occurs, in part, by each bird's different voice.

LAUGHING GULL *(L. ATRICILLA)*: Laughing gulls are the smallest of the three gulls mentioned. They have a white breast and gray wings like the herring gull, but a black head and tail tip. They have not bounced back as well as the other gull species. With a keen eye, you may occasionally see them around Mount Desert Island. Their high-pitched cry is the source of their name.

TERNS *(STERNA)*: Of the three terns in this area, the common tern *(S. hirundo)* is more frequently seen than the arctic tern *(S. paradisaea)* or roseate tern *(S. dougallii)*. Terns have coloring similar to that of laughing gulls (without the black tail tip) but are smaller, with slender bodies, pointed wings, and forked tails. Their graceful flight, quick wing beats, and tail shape differentiate them from gulls. Highly adapted for flying, terns are extremely poor swimmers.

Commonly called "sea swallows," terns are known for their tremendous migrations. The arctic tern migrates from the Maine islands east across the Atlantic to Europe and down the west coast of Africa to the Antarctic Ocean, where it spends its second summer. A total of 22,000 miles, the trip is almost equivalent to a complete circumnavigation of the Earth. With an average life span of 15 to 40 years, terns cover a lot of miles!

Terns are very social and live in large colonies. In 1886, sixty-seven Maine islands had colonies of terns, and they were one of the most abundant seabirds. Like other species, by 1900 they were almost wiped out; up to 100,000 were killed in a season and 1,200 were reported killed in a single day. Under protection, terns increased in number, and

the population became stable in the 1940s. But by the 1950s, it began to slowly decline again. Their numbers continued to drop throughout the 1970s, until an aggressive protection movement began in the early 1980s. Since 1984, the arctic tern population has increased by 67 percent and the common and roseate tern populations by more than 100 percent. Unfortunately, though these numbers show an increase in the entire tern population, colonies are still almost nonexistent on islands that are not protected and managed.

The decline is due to human disturbance, such as coastal and island development, and the exploding gull population. During the latter half of May, when the terns arrive to nest and lay eggs, they are very susceptible to disturbance and predation by gulls. Some ornithologists believe that without even more aggressive protection, terns are headed toward extinction.

DOUBLE-CRESTED CORMORANT (*PHALACROCORAX AURITUS*): Almost as common as gulls, cormorants are all black, with long necks and tails. They are distinguished from loons by having bodies that sit lower in the water, longer necks, and heads that are tilted slightly upward when the birds rest in the water.

Cormorants are also known as lawyer birds, crow ducks, sea ravens, and, locally, shags. Their Latin name comes from words meaning "crow." Related to the pelican, frigate bird, gannet, and boobie, the cormorant is a very primitive bird. The young are born with reptile-like scales rather than feathers. The excrement, or guano, of cormorants is so acidic that often islands with nesting colonies have only the skeletons of trees remaining among the nests. The Thrumcap, a small island south of the Porcupines in Frenchman Bay, is an example.

Cormorants have heavier skeletons than most other birds, whose bones are hollow and porous. Also, cormorant feathers have fewer cross-hatches, which makes them less waterproof, so cormorants are often seen standing with wings outstretched to dry their feathers and thermoregulate. When they take off to fly, cormorants run on top of the water before becoming airborne.

While these adaptations might seem disadvantageous for a bird, they enable the cormorant to be a spectacular swimmer—diving as much as 100 feet underwater. They are still used in some Asian countries to catch fish. The bird is tied to a leash and sent out diving. A band around its neck prevents it from swallowing its catch.

Cormorants are still killed by American and Canadian fishermen who believe that the birds eat fish from weirs and pens. The birds actually are said to prefer bottom dwellers, or "trash fish," such as sculpin, cunner, and gunnel. Cormorant chicks and eggs are also very susceptible to predation if adults are flushed from the nest. According to some studies, even a 10-minute interval of exposure can result in a greater than 20 percent loss of eggs.

BLACK GUILLEMOT *(CEPPHUS GRYLLE)*: My favorite bird of all, the black guillemot, is a common resident around Mount Desert Island, particularly in Frenchman Bay. With its small, tublike black body and white wing patch, it looks like a little strobe light as it flies by. It has little bright red feet. If you're lucky enough to see one yawn, you will see that the inside of its mouth is also bright red, the same color as its favorite food, the red rock eel. Known as sea doves, sea pigeons, and locally as squeaks because of their call, guillemots remind me of rubber-duckies, noise and all.

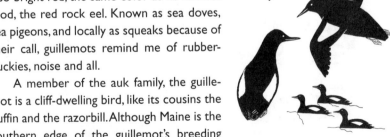

A member of the auk family, the guillemot is a cliff-dwelling bird, like its cousins the puffin and the razorbill. Although Maine is the southern edge of the guillemot's breeding range, it is able to live and reproduce here because of the cold, rich waters. Like the penguin's, the guillemot's body shape and short wings allow it to dive through the water with quick maneuverability and speed.

The guillemot's almost nonexistent nest is located under rocks or on cliffs; the eggs are oval or cone-shaped to prevent them from rolling off the cliff.

Several factors threaten the guillemot today, including oil pollution, human disturbance, and overfishing. Additionally, great black-backed and herring gulls eat guillemot eggs and populate previous nesting sites. Currently there are 116 islands on the Maine coast occupied by guillemots, with eleven of the colonies having more than 100 breeding pairs. These birds, like the tern, are under strict and aggressive protection.

PUFFINS *(FRATERCULA ARCTICA)*: I mention puffins not because you'll ever see any around Mount Desert Island (except in the many gift shops), but because most people *want* to see puffins.

The common puffin, also known as the sea parrot, spends two years at sea before returning in the spring of its third year to breed on the island where it was born. Nests are usually burrows in the ground. Puffins used to occupy six islands on the Maine coast, but as with other seabirds, their population declined. By 1902, there was only one pair found in Maine. Today, there are more than 1,200 puffins nesting on Matinicus Rock, Petit Manan, Machias Seal Island, and Eastern Egg Rock, largely due to the Puffin Project. This aggressive program to reintroduce puffins in their former breeding colonies began in 1973. Today, there are boat trips for the public to see and learn more about the puffin; one such trip leaves from Bar Harbor.

COMMON EIDER *(SOMATERIA MOLLISSIMA)*: Maine and Alaska are the only places in the United States where eiders nest. Around Mount Desert

Island, I have most often seen these birds while kayaking in Frenchman Bay. Males have a white body with black wings; females are mottled brown. The eider is the largest duck in North America, weighing between three and a half, and five and a half pounds. It is about the size of a gull but slightly fatter and squatter. Its name comes from the classic Greek words for "body" and "wool," referring to its thick down.

As ducks, eiders have very different life histories from those of other seabirds. For example, only the female tends the eggs. She does not leave the nest, even to eat, and relies on her fat deposits for energy. The drakes stay off the island in bachelor parties, taking no role in raising the offspring. When you are kayaking, you can often see groups of only males flying together.

If the eggs escape predation, the newly hatched chicks are herded down to the water within twenty-four hours, under cover of darkness. Raising the chicks is a communal effort, as several females and their chicks band together into a large group for better protection from predators. A complicated social structure exists among the adult ducks, who, for the next sixty to sixty-five days, take turns caring for the flotilla of chicks. Females and chicks are sometimes seen around Mount Desert Island in late summer.

In late August, both the males and females move offshore and molt. Whereas most birds lose a feather at a time, eiders lose all their feathers at once, leaving them flightless. It was during this season that market hunters often drove the eiders onto shore by the thousands, almost wiping out entire colonies at a time; one report states that in 1904 there were only four adults on the Maine coast. Through aggressive protection from the National Audubon Society, by the 1940s eiders increased to 2,000 nesting pairs and by 1967 to 18,000 nesting pairs. Currently, there are 22,000 nesting pairs on 239 Maine islands.

Like all seabirds, eiders are easily disturbed by human presence, particularly during their nesting season and when the chicks are young (between early May and mid-August). Most pertinent for the kayaker is to avoid disturbing the floating rafts of females and chicks, for gulls can swoop in and grab unguarded chicks instantly.

COMMON LOON *(GAVIA IMMER)*: As it is for many other northern birds, the coast of Maine is the southern edge of the breeding range for loons. They are excellent divers, second only to the penguin, and have been caught in fishing nets more than 200 feet deep. Loons summer and nest on inland lakes, then migrate to coastal waters in winter. Around Mount Desert Island, you will occasionally see loons in the middle of summer, though the more probable times

are spring or fall. They often have their winter plumage of brown feathers at this time.

Their dark summer plumage is similar to that of a cormorant seen at a distance. The key to positive identification is the loon's higher body position in the water, head that is held level compared to the upward tilt of the cormorant's, and white breast patch. Interestingly, the loon's name comes not from their strange call but from the Shetland word for "lame," referring to their awkwardness on land.

GREAT BLUE HERON *(ARDEA HERODIAS)*: Herons have occupied this area since pre-Colonial times, as indicated by the many Heron Islands along the coast. Unfortunately, herons were also hunted for their dramatic plumes, and the population was severely depleted by the turn of the century. The National Audubon Society helped reestablish this bird, and currently fourteen significant Maine coastal colonies exist.

The great blue heron is the largest member of the heron family. It can stand up to four feet high with a wingspan of six feet. A migratory bird, it winters in the southern United States and returns north to the same nest in April. Herons prefer to nest near marshes, grassland, and shallow waters, making their large nest on the top of the tallest tree, fifty to one hundred feet in the air. Several nests may occupy the same tree. Herons nest in colonies of up to 150 pairs but are most often seen flying alone.

There are no nesting colonies in the Mount Desert Island area, but herons can be sighted at Mount Desert Narrows, Bar Island in Frenchman Bay, and Bartlett Narrows in Blue Hill Bay.

OSPREY *(PANDION HALIAETUS)*: This bird of prey, also called the sea hawk or fish hawk, has a streamlined body about the size of a herring gull's yet with a wingspan of four to six feet. It is a boldly marked bird, mostly dark brown on the top and mottled white on the bottom. The osprey has hooked feet and a prominent elbow on its wings, which appear sickle-shaped when in flight. As with all birds of prey, the female is larger than the male.

Osprey are present on every continent except Antarctica. Those which summer in North America spend the winter in Central or South America and return to the same nest in April. They prefer to nest in high trees, as do herons and eagles, though some nests are built on rock outcroppings or ledges, such as the nest on Sutton Island near the Cranberry Islands. Humans also unintentionally provide favored nesting sites on navigational buoys, day beacons, and utility poles. In the last year or so I have noticed a great increase in osprey sightings and nesting sites. While I used to see osprey mostly in Bartlett Narrows, I now see them all over Mount Desert Island.

Like all birds of prey, the osprey has suffered from the effects of DDT, but it was one of the few birds not severely affected during the fashion craze for feathers at the turn of the century. They were apparently protected by an old superstition that bad luck would follow those taking the life of an osprey. Thank goodness for folklore.

AMERICAN BALD EAGLE (*HALIAEETUS LEUCOCEPHALUS*): Last, but not least, we come to the majestic symbol of our country. Larger than a great black-backed gull (though the two can be mistaken for each other at a distance), the eagle has a body length of well over two feet. Its wingspan is six to eight feet, making it quite a sight to see. The body of a mature eagle is dark brown with a characteristic white head and tail tip. To differentiate an eagle from a great black-backed gull, watch how frequently they flap their wings; eagles tend to soar much more than gulls do. To differentiate an eagle from an osprey,

osprey

eagle

look for the straighter wing and solid body color of the eagle compared to the hooked elbow and mottled white underside of the osprey. I have seen eagles in every paddling area around greater Mount Desert Island.

Eagles are monogamous and usually mate for life. They court and build their nest in February and lay their eggs in April. The chicks hatch approximately a month later and begin to fledge (grow their flight feathers and leave the nest) between mid-June and mid-August. Two-thirds of the eagles in Maine live on the coast, half of those on islands.

It is currently being recommended that eagles be down-listed from the status of "endangered" to "threatened" in the northeastern U.S., but in Maine, at least, the productivity rates are below the one-hatchling-per-nest benchmark that the Maine Endangered Species Act defines as "reproductive success." While the eagle population in the Mount Desert Island area is increasing, it is doing so more slowly than populations in other parts of the state.

A bald eagle near Bartlett Island, photographed with a telephoto lens.
W. DAVID ANDREWS II.

Between 1960 and 1974, only seven young eagles in the Mount Desert Island area survived to adulthood. In 1975 there were twelve monitored nests, five of which were occupied. Two chicks were hatched, resulting in a productivity rate of .4 young per nest, compared to .35 per nest statewide. Seventeen years later, in 1992, there were nineteen nests, fourteen of which were occupied. The productivity rate was .64 (nine eaglets hatched), compared to a rate of .81 statewide. In 1995 the productivity rate for the Mount Desert area was .55, compared to .92 statewide and 1.2 for the other northern states.

A number of studies are underway to determine why Maine has fewer eagles than other northern states, and several theories have been proposed. The first theory is that eagles are being harmed by environmental contamination. At the top of the food chain, toxins bioaccumulate and reach high concentrations in eagles' tissues. Maine eagles have been found to have relatively high levels of dioxins, PCBs, and DDE, chemicals that interfere with hormone levels and result in poor reproduction, thin eggshells that break under the bird's weight, dead embryos, and poor survival of young. The most likely source of many of these pollutants is the papermaking industry, which releases dioxins and furans into Maine rivers.

Another possible explanation is habitat loss and human disturbance. Studies have shown that eagles will move their nest sites to avoid human disturbance near their nest or feeding territory. Disturbance from the water, it is suggested, is more detrimental than that from land; boaters should stay a minimum of one quarter to one-half mile from the nest and also avoid feeding grounds. (Our most beneficial behavior around eagles is summarized in the chapter on environmental kayaking.)

Lastly, eagles sometimes fly into powerlines, and a number of illegal shootings and trappings occur every year.

MARINE MAMMALS

There is something about mammals that live in the sea, something that intrigues us, fascinates us, and connects us. These warm-blooded animals, though they spend their lives in oceanic waters, have life histories similar to ours. They bear live young and nurse them with milk, have strong interpersonal bonds, communicate with complex vocalizations, and are intellectually advanced, allowing for free time to play, frolic, and explore. These brothers and sisters of the sea have captured the imagination and affection of humans for many generations. The Gulf of Maine supports a variety of marine mammals, of which you might see four: the harbor seal, gray seal, harbor porpoise, and minke whale.

SEALS. These highly intelligent animals can remain underwater from five to forty minutes and dive 650 feet. When diving, their heart rate drops from eighty to ten beats per minute, with blood supplied primarily to the brain. Seals can swim between six and sixteen miles per hour. I think of the many times I have sat in my boat trying to figure out where a seal would next surface, when it was probably already miles away!

Seals are accused of destroying fishing gear and eating valuable fish; as a result, they were (and still are) shot by some fishermen and lobstermen. Massachusetts did not lift its bounty on harbor seals until 1962. Seals do carry cod worm, a parasite that lives its adult stage in the seals' stomach and its larval stage in the gut and muscles of codfish, making the fish unmarketable. However, even when seals were not protected and their population was declining, the cod worm epidemic continued.

Telling the difference between a seal head and a lobster buoy is a fine art. My advice is to watch the water surface. If the dark floating object eventually disappears, it was a seal; if not, it's a buoy. You may spot harbor seals or gray seals while kayaking around Mount Desert Island, but harbor seals are much more commonly seen.

HARBOR SEALS (*PHOCA VITULINA*): Widely distributed throughout the world, harbor seals grow to approximately five feet long and weigh be-

tween 150 and 200 pounds. They range in color from gray to black and tan to brown, usually with mottled fur, although this is hard to see from a kayak. Male and female harbor seals are close in

size, weight, and color, making it extremely difficult to distinguish the two. Seals make many sounds, including flipper slapping, bubble blowing, growling, snorting, gurgling, and burping. Their scientific name means "sea calf" or "sea dog," which aids in their identification: if it is cute and adorable, it is a harbor seal.

Seals usually haul out on rock ledges during low tide and feed in the water during high tide. Being opportunistic carnivores, seals eat a large variety of food, including fish (rockfish, herring, cod, mackerel, flounder and salmon), mollusks (squid, clams, and octopus), crustaceans (crabs and shrimp) and seabirds (ducks and guillemots). They sometimes feed cooperatively, diving and herding fish. They eat up to 6 percent of their body weight a day and can live up to thirty years.

Seal pups, born between April and June, are approximately two and a half feet long, and weigh an average of twenty pounds. Pup mortality during the first year is around 28 percent. During the first few weeks of life, pups are completely dependent on their mothers' milk as they store up extra layers of body fat to support them when they are weaned and learning to fish. The bond between mother and pup is strong; they recognize each other through smell and voice.

After the Marine Mammal Protection Act was passed in 1972, the Maine harbor seal population grew from 5,800 to 14,500 in 1986. In 1993 there were 28,800 harbor seals in the Gulf of Maine.

It is important for kayakers to always avoid disturbing seals that are hauled out on land. This is especially critical during the pupping season (April to July) and molting season (July and August). Kayaks, more than other boats, seem to elicit panic among seal colonies. The chapter on environmental kayaking further explains the effect of our actions as kayakers.

GRAY SEAL *(HALICHOERUS GRYPUS)*: The gray seal, not as cute or social as the harbor seal, is also less common. It is currently thought that only 400 gray seals live in coastal Maine waters, making them relatively uncommon. Maine is near the southern end of their breeding range.

Kayaking around the Mount Desert Island area, though, you will have a fairly good chance of seeing one. The easiest way to tell them from harbor seals is to remember that their scientific name means "hook-nosed pig of the sea." You'll easily discern their horse-like head and flaring nostrils. Males grow to eight feet and 1,000 pounds; females reach seven feet and weigh 600 pounds. Males live to thirty-five years, females to forty-five years. Gray seals are somewhat darker than harbor seals and mottled with larger spots. The diet of a gray seal is similar to that of a harbor seal.

Gray seal pups are born from December through February and have a mortality rate of 30 to 55 percent, often due to predation by

sharks. Since gray seals stay farther offshore than harbor seals, pups are much less susceptible to human disturbance. Gray seals usually cause less havoc for fishermen and have been hunted less than the curious harbor seal, although Canada began paying a bounty on gray seals in 1976 because they also carry cod worm.

HARBOR PORPOISE *(PHOCOENA PHOCOENA)*: Harbor porpoises are actually toothed whales. They are the smallest whale, at five feet and 140 pounds, and the shortest lived, at ten years. During the early spring, porpoises often travel alone or in pairs; in summer and fall, larger groups of twenty or more will travel together.

The best way to find a harbor porpoise is to sit and listen carefully. If one is in the vicinity, you will hear a soft puff, without the visible spout emitted by other whales. This breathing sound is the source of the local name "puffers" or "puffing pigs." After the puff, look for a triangular dorsal fin that curves slightly at its trailing edge. Once you have spotted the porpoise, count the number of surfacings. It will usually surface three to four times before making a longer deep dive lasting for several minutes.

I once saw a group of approximately forty porpoises feeding together during the summer in Frenchman Bay. Heading toward Sheep Porcupine, we paddled into the middle of a school of fish that had congregated in the channel. Porpoises began breaching and jumping all around us; we were being sprayed by their splashes. Preoccupied with the feeding frenzy, one porpoise almost bumped a kayak.

Porpoises usually swim quickly by large or moving boats. They will, however, sometimes swim close to observe a stopped and quiet kayak, especially if it happens to be floating above a school of fish.

There are currently 45,000 to 65,000 harbor porpoises in the Gulf of Maine and Bay of Fundy. They eat herring, mackerel, cod, redfish, and squid, but their most important food source, herring, was severely over-

dorsal fins

fished during the 1970s. Due to entanglement in fishing nets, competition with fisheries for food, and coastal pollution, their mortality rate is dramatically increasing. Off the coast of Maine, approximately 1,250 individuals a year are caught and killed in gill nets alone. Porpoises also drown due to encounters with plastic bags, balloons, fishing gear, and other garbage.

Porpoise body tissue has also been found to contain high levels of pesticides (DDT), heavy metals (especially mercury), and PCBs. In the 1960s, a porpoise in this area was found to have the highest level of mercury and DDT ever recorded in a wild animal. In Canada, the porpoise is on the "threatened" list, and it has been proposed that the same action be taken in the United States.

A commonly asked question is the difference between a dolphin and a porpoise. Dolphins and porpoises belong to separate families (just as cats and dogs are from different taxonomic families). Porpoises have flattened teeth, a blunt noise, and small triangular fins. The word *porpoise* originates from two Latin words meaning "pig" and "fish"; porpoises were known for their succulent meat. Dolphins are bigger than porpoises. They have pointed teeth and large curved fins. The word *dolphin* comes from a Greek word meaning "womb." These animals have always been considered holy. White-sided and white-beaked dolphins live far offshore in the Gulf of Maine, so the chances of seeing one while paddling shallow coastal waters are slim.

MINKE WHALES (*BALAENOPTERA ACUTOROSTRATA*): Minkes are the smallest of the baleen whales, ranging from fifteen to thirty feet. They weigh eleven tons and can live up to fifty years. Unlike some other whale species, minkes rarely breach or show flukes; because of their body shape and weight distribution, they do not need the added momentum before diving. They also do not make a visible blow or spout. They often swim alone and are most often sighted during the summer.

dorsal fin

Until recently, minkes were the most abundant and most heavily harvested baleen whale. Penobscot and Passamaquoddy Indians used to hunt them from canoes. Greenland Eskimos are currently allowed to kill up to 115 a year for food, there is a traditional annual hunt in Iceland, and the Japanese still kill a significant number each year.

When minke whales surface for air, their pointed snout often breaks the surface first, followed by their crescent-shaped dorsal fin. Like porpoises, they usually breathe two or three times at intervals of thirty seconds before taking a deep dive for two to three minutes, though they have been known to hold their breath for up to twenty minutes. Observing this breathing pattern will allow you to better predict when and where an individual might surface.

The first time I saw a minke whale it appeared seemingly out of nowhere. It looked big and hard—I really didn't want to get hit by it—yet graceful, dancing through the water, knowing exactly where I was. With a straight, pointed fin pushing aside the water, followed by the full length of its body, it headed slowly in my direction. As it slipped beneath the surface, the air was still, the water was flat, and nothing moved except the beast under my boat. Time seemed to stop; I didn't look down.

What happens when an animal the size of a Greyhound bus surfaces next to you? Sometimes minkes simply swim by boats, minding their own business; other times they approach for a closer look. Although minkes are relatively safe to paddle near, I always try to respect the animal's space and feeding activity. After sighting a minke, I stop paddling and stay where I am; I let the whale approach me—if it chooses. It will sometimes swim closer, circling the kayaks, swimming between or under boats before swimming off, returning to previous activities. I have seen minkes surfacing within five to ten feet of a boat.

There have been no reports of whales swimming under boats and purposely turning them over. In fact, whales know your location far better than you know theirs and—unless given reason—have no cause to harm you. There have, however, been a handful of cases in which small research boats, skiffs, and kayaks were flipped by whales breaching (minkes rarely breach) and tail slapping (minkes do not tail slap). Although you should always remember, "Small, silent boats should not linger near large, leaping whales,"[2] my best advice, should you be so fortunate as to be approached closely by a whale, is to relax, enjoy it, and give a special thank-you to Mother Nature.

---

2. Steve Katona, Valerie Rough, and David Richardson, *A Field Guide to Whales, Porpoises, and Seals.* p. 20

Social History

*The sea is possessed by its own mood and spirits,
and men and women are almost nothing to it.*

PHILIP CONKLING

I find it fascinating, as I paddle to my favorite patches of rock and vegetation, to think of all that these islands have witnessed before me and all that they will witness after I leave. The islands have seen humans follow a course of reliance on the sea and utilization of her resources,

The Mount Desert Island ferry wharf, 1886.
BAR HARBOR HISTORICAL SOCIETY.

from the first Native American oceangoing boats, to the ships of early explorers, to the development of permanent island communities, to the current trend toward island preservation and conservation. The islands will outlast us by many hundreds of thousands of years and will witness events that have yet to unfold. We are only a chapter in their history, as they are a chapter in ours.

Many books on the coastal, maritime, and social history of Maine exist; those useful for the kayaker are listed in the bibliography. This chapter presents a very abridged version of Maine's social history, paying particular attention to the Mount Desert Island area and people's interactions with the sea and islands nearby.

THE FIRST INHABITANTS

What archaeologists know about the history of Maine's first inhabitants comes in part from the 1,500 shell heaps, or middens, found along the coast. Shell middens are Native American garbage dumps in which centuries-old refuse has been preserved by the neutralizing effect of the soft-shelled clam and mussel shells piled therein. The middens reveal much about the life and diet of the native peoples. For example, almost all middens are located near a cobble or sand beach that is accessible at all tides, and often close to a clam flat. This is true of both shell middens around Mount Desert Island—one on Thomas Island, the other on Bartlett Island.

The first native peoples were the Paleo-Indians, who lived in Maine from approximately 9500 to 7500 B.C. They survived mostly by hunting large land mammals. In 6000 B.C. the Early Archaic Indians arrived, and were the first inhabitants to utilize both freshwater and marine food sources.

By 2000 B.C. the Red Paint People were living along the Maine coast. Their name comes from the red ochre (a clay stained with iron oxide) found in their graves. In addition to collecting food on or near shore, the Red Paint People fished far offshore in canoes or similar boats carved from massive tree trunks.

The Ceramic Group lived in this area around 500 B.C. They made ceramic pots and bowls, an activity that anthropologists believe marks the beginnings of agriculture. These migratory people spent summers fishing on the coast and islands and winters hunting inland. They relied heavily on the sea for food and traded with other groups.

Next came the Abenakis, a nation still prominent in New England today. The Abenakis were also migratory, using canoes of sophisticated design and construction as their primary mode of transportation. Their light, durable, easy-to-handle craft were made from elm, spruce, oak, pine, and chestnut, animal skins, and—most familiar—birch bark. (Today's famous Old Town canoes, built near Bangor, are modeled after Abenaki designs.) Some of their canoes, large enough to hold forty people, were designed for coastal travel and were used for hunting seals, porpoises, and whales. Although it is debated whether these coastal Native Americans had the capacity to sail before European contact, by 1600, early explorers reported seeing sailing canoes with covered decks.

The Abbe museum, in Acadia National Park, is a good place to learn more about Native Americans in Maine.

EUROPEAN VISITORS

It is widely believed by historians that Vikings led by Leif Ericson, son of Eric the Red, were the first European visitors to North America. They arrived around 1000 A.D., sailing from Greenland in search of lumber. Writing in his ship's log, Leif the Lucky told of a long inlet flanked by mountains on either side, with a meadow nearby, where he and his crew landed for the first time in what we now call North America. Many communities, from the Canadian Provinces to Cape Cod, have claimed to be the site of Ericson's first footprints in the New World. Even Mount Desert Island might qualify, for any boater entering Somes Sound can clearly see the scene Ericson described.

For 400 years after Ericson's landing, the islands were visited and used only by the Abenakis. When the second wave of Europeans arrived, from the late 1400s to the early 1600s, this area saw a substantial increase in use and visitation. Cadillac Mountain—at 1,530 feet, one of the highest peaks on the East Coast—can be seen from sixty miles out at sea on a clear day and has been a significant landmark for both early and present-day sailors.

Explorers were the first Europeans to come. Portuguese and Italian sailors began to visit and chart the Gulf of Maine. French, English, and Spanish explorers followed, all seeking the northwest passage to the Orient. Then came the treasure hunters, fishermen, fur traders, and loggers. Last to arrive were those seeking religious freedom and land.

Samuel de Champlain, a geographer sailing to establish French control in America, was the first documented explorer to actually hit Mount Desert Island—literally. On September 5, 1604, he ran aground on a shoal off Otter Point and was forced to stay while his ship was repaired. Champlain called the area La Cadie, a word adapted from the Abenaki suffix *akade*, meaning "where it is plentiful." The name eventually became L'Acadie, and then Acadia, as we know it today. Champlain also named the island *L'Isle des Monts Deserts*, meaning "Island of the Desert [or Barren] Mountains," because of the bald mountain summits and steep cliffs. The name remains Mount Desert Island (with the accent on the second syllable), and Champlain's visit is commemorated by Mt. Champlain, located within Acadia National Park.

After the European "discovery" of America, treasure-seekers arrived in search of gold and silver. Eventually, what author Bill Caldwell calls the "true silver mines of Maine" were recognized: the area's rich fisheries. In 1600, as many as 300 foreign fishing vessels worked the waters of Maine, supplying the very high demand for seafood and fish in Europe. Other resources such as lumber were soon utilized as well. Tall, straight trees were needed for masts on ships; any white pine greater than twenty-four inches in diameter was deemed the property of the king of England and became known as King's Pine.

ISLAND SETTLEMENTS

Mount Desert Island's first permanent settlement was started in 1613 and marked the site of the first bloodshed between the English and the French in the New World. French Jesuit priests Father Biard and Father Masse landed at the mouth of Somes Sound at Fernald Point and formed a colony called St. Sauveur. The priests, who intended to convert the "savages," successfully baptized the Abenaki chief, Asticou, before their colony was destroyed by the English. The Asticou Inn, in Northeast Harbor, and St. Sauveur Mountain preserve these historical names.

The French and English continued to fight over the New England coast for the next 150 years, making settlement along the Maine coast and islands both difficult and dangerous. The conflict culminated in the French and Indian War (1754–63). By the end of the war, a few small year-round communities were established, several of them in Blue Hill Bay. Around the turn of the nineteenth century, the island populations began to increase, and by 1830 seventy-five islands in Penobscot Bay and Blue Hill Bay alone were inhabited.

The early islanders, like those of today, were self-sufficient, independent, resourceful, and highly diversified in their abilities. This lifestyle is said to be a major ingredient of the down east character. Fishing, lumbering, and boatbuilding were the main island trades. Hay was sold inland, and small factories pressed pogy oil. (Pogies are a schooling fish, like mackerel and herring.) Lobster was sold commercially for the first time in 1850, and by 1897 there were 142 licensed lobstermen in Maine. The development of this industry lowered lobster populations almost immediately, and the first size regulations were adopted by the turn of the twentieth century. In down east Maine, island farming was rarely profitable and was usually practiced only for subsistence. Ironbound Island in Frenchman Bay and Bartlett Island in Blue Hill Bay were two exceptions.

During the second half of the nineteenth century, a significant quarrying industry developed on the islands, and by 1890 Maine led the country in granite production. Thirty-three Maine islands had quarries, including Hall Quarry on upper Somes Sound on Mount Desert Island. Several factors led the almost overnight shutdown of most island quarries in the early 1900s, however. Cement replaced granite for construction, government contracts ended, and railroads began to replace coastal shipping as the principal means of transporting freight. Boomtowns turned into ghost towns; on Hurricane Island, in Penobscot Bay, quarrymen's families literally left set dinner tables to catch the last ferry off the island. No other in-

An abandoned quarry on Mount Desert Island.
W. DAVID ANDREWS II.

dustry has left such an irreversible, permanent mark on Maine islands as quarrying.

The limited resources and physical isolation of island living resulted in communities that were highly interdependent. Islanders pooled their resources and labor in difficult times; provided their own entertainment with dances, games, and other social events; and often found their marriage partners on their own or nearby islands. Providing schooling for island children required a community effort. A teacher brought from the mainland would be housed for short periods with each family. If there were not enough pupils for their own schools, several island communities might combine their students to fill one school.

As with schools, it was rare to have a church on an island, and difficulty of travel limited the amount of communally practiced religion. The interdenominational Maine Seacoast Mission was founded in 1905 "to undertake religious and benevolent work with the people in the neglected communities and among the isolated families along the coast and on the islands." To this day, the Seacoast Mission, whose vessel, the *Sunbeam*, is headquartered in Bar Harbor, provides an array of services, from bringing ministers, teachers, and much-needed company, to delivering food, clothing, and presents for the holidays. The Seacoast Mission is Maine's Red Cross of the sea.

In the early twentieth century, island populations began to decline. With expanding roads and railroads on the mainland, the islands lost their transportation advantages. In addition, the state made secondary-school attendance mandatory. Parents were faced with the choice of either moving their entire family to the mainland or sending their teenagers to board on the mainland while they attended school. This accelerated the depopulation of islands, and by the end of World War II, most islands were uninhabited.

THE CLAIMING AND SETTLEMENT OF MOUNT DESERT ISLAND

In the late 1700s, a French and an English family both claimed ownership of Mount Desert Island. Marie Therese de la Mothe Cadillac de Gregoire (granddaughter of a Frenchman who had lived in Hulls Cove and was given Mount Desert Island by Louis XIV in 1689) claimed

Mount Desert Street, Bar Harbor, in 1876.
BAR HARBOR HISTORICAL SOCIETY.

Mount Desert Island by inheritance. The English son of Sir Francis Bernard claimed Mount Desert Island based on a grant in 1762 from the Massachusetts Bay Colony. Thomas Jefferson settled the dispute in 1787 by dividing the island and granting Cadillac's descendants the eastern half and the Cranberry Islands, and Bernard's descendants the western half. This is easy to remember because Cadillac Mountain is on the east side of Mount Desert Island, and Bernard Mountain is on the west.

The first white settler to establish permanent residency on Mount Desert Island, Abraham Somes, arrived from Gloucester, Massachusetts, in 1759. He was given land at the top of Somes Sound by the Massachusetts Bay Colony, and by the 1770s a small town called Somesville was established. You can see the town and first landing site while paddling in Somes Harbor in Upper Somes Sound.

THE GROWTH OF BAR HARBOR

While the early histories of many Maine island settlements followed similar patterns, the development of Bar Harbor took a vastly different turn in 1837, when easy access to the mainland was provided by a bridge built from Mount Desert Island to the mainland.

In 1844, Thomas Cole, a famous painter of the Hudson River school, visited Mount Desert Island, in part due to its accessibility. Cole continually raved about the paradise of Mount Desert Island: "Sand Beach Head, the eastern extremity of Mount Desert Island, is a tremendous overhanging precipice, rising from the ocean, with the surf dashing against it in a frightful manner. The coast along here is iron bound—threatening crags, and dark caverns in which the sea thunders. The view

Thomas Cole, **View across Frenchman Bay from Mount Desert Island after a Squall.** *Oil on canvas.*
CINCINNATI ART MUSEUM

of Frenchman's bay and island is truly fine. Some of the islands, called porcupines, are lofty, and belted with crags which glitter in the setting sun. Beyond and across the bay is a range of mountains of beautiful aerial hues." [1]

Other painters and artists soon arrived. Following the artists came the wealthy of Boston and New York, wanting to see this "Eden" for themselves. By the 1890s, these "rusticators" had transformed Bar Harbor into the summer social capital of the United States. Debutantes had summer romances; dances and concerts were held; horse races and boat regattas filled the days. Social gatherings and status were priorities. The wealthy summer residents built huge, lavish "cottages," some staffed by as many as forty servants. Paddlers can still see several of these man-

Three rusticators sailing from Northeast Harbor to Long Island, c. 1900.
NORTHEAST HARBOR LIBRARY.

1. John Wilmerding, *The Artist's Mount Desert,* p. 28.

Ink drawings by "Crayon Quill" of rusticators enjoying the shore, 1873.
NORTHEAST HARBOR LIBRARY.

sions along the Shore Path and West Street near Bar Island in Frenchman Bay. The ironically named rusticators created a lifestyle that was far
from simple and quiet.

Around the turn of the century, however,
as transportation improved and more and
more people came for short visits, summer
residents were soon outnumbered by vacationers. Concerned by the increasing number
of visitors and the increased lumbering activity
on the islands, George Bucknam Dorr and Dr.
Charles Eliot began a movement in 1901 to establish a national park. Along with other well-
to-do individuals, they bought land and donated
it to the government, creating the Sieur de
Monts National Monument in 1916. In 1919,
the land became Lafayette National Park, the
first national park east of the Mississippi and
the only one to be privately bought and donated to the park service. This step was the
first in a movement of land preservation and
conservation, particularly by private individuals,
that is currently very strong along the Maine

*George Dorr atop
Dorr Mountain,
date unknown.*
BAR HARBOR HISTORICAL SOCIETY.

coast. Amusingly, the name of the park was changed to Acadia when an
English family donated Schoodic Peninsula to the park in 1929 but ob-

jected to the French name Lafayette. Evidently they didn't know that the name Acadia was given to this area in 1604 by Champlain, a Frenchman.

The Depression of the 1930s, the establishment of the income tax, and World War II all took a toll on the rusticators' lifestyles. Many of the great summer "cottages" were already vacant and falling into disrepair even before a fire raged across part of Mount Desert Island in October 1947. More than half of the town of Bar Harbor, including 237 houses and many mansions, burned to the ground. The infamous Fire of '47 burned, mostly uncontrolled, for twenty-nine days, destroying $2 million in property and more than 17,000 acres of shoreline and mountainsides.

CHANGING VALUE OF ISLANDS

Throughout the last two hundred years, islands have been, at different times, both ignored or greatly desired real estate. When Maine still belonged to Massachusetts, that state tried, with little luck, to sell the "troublesome" islands to private buyers. After gaining independence in 1820, Maine also tried to sell the islands. Yet, over the next fifty-five years, only 109 islands were sold. Finally, in 1876, the state held a mass auction and sold 66 islands at prices up to $450; most went for $25. Black Island, just north of Bartlett Island in Blue Hill Bay, sold for a whopping $10.

This was to change, however, beginning in the 1880s when the first "island fever" took hold. Island populations began to grow, and the state government was swamped with inquires about buying islands. Because the state, and most islanders for that matter, did not know who owned which islands—earlier settlers lived on the islands for generations without ever establishing ownership—the state in 1913 claimed title to all islands not held in private ownership.

From the 1930s to the 1950s, as island populations declined and residents moved inland, islands again sold cheaply. In the '60s and '70s there was another island rush that has continued to the present. The same small island that would have sold for $3,500 in 1950 cost $35,000 in 1960 and $200,000 in the 1980s.

In 1974, the state again set out to clarify the ambiguous ownership of the islands of Maine. The Coastal Island Registry was founded, resulting in the registration of 1,700 privately owned and 1,299 unregistered, and therefore state-owned, islands. Today, such organizations as The Nature Conservancy, Maine Coast Heritage Trust, Acadia National Park, Island Institute, and Maine Audubon Society are devoted to preserving and caring for Maine's islands. Most of this is accomplished through land preserves and easements.

Another organization, the Maine Island Trail Association, has played its part by developing a 325-mile route from Portland to Machias. Consisting of more than seventy islands, the trail is most often traveled by kayakers. The organization is "committed to preserving Maine's undeveloped islands in their natural state while providing a recreational asset for responsible visitors . . . by encouraging a sense of stewardship and promoting a philosophy of low-impact use among its members. The association also strives to educate island visitors about low-impact practices, natural history, and ecological sensitivity."[2]

Maine waters have been paddled for a long time and will continue to be. Following in the wake of the first tree-trunk canoes, all of us who paddle are participants in a long history of self-propelled ocean exploration and transportation. The Maine Island Trail is an excellent example of how our view of islands has evolved in this century. As ever more people explore the islands and waters of Mount Desert, it is crucial that we understand how history has shaped the islands we visit today and how crucial our role will be in their future.

2. Maine Island Trail 1995 guidebook, p. 4.

Environmental Kayaking

What is required is an act of faith on the one hand and an acceptance of an ethic on the other. Faith that people can be trusted must be instilled in the minds of private property owners, public land managers, and other guardians of desirable landscape, while users must adopt an ethic that includes a heavy dollop of stewardship for all land and a willingness to abide by rules when not being watched.

DAVID GETCHELL, SR.

As Leslie Cowperthwaite, director of Maine Seal (a nonprofit research organization) noted, "By and large . . . kayakers are conscientious and conservation-minded people who care deeply about the natural world and its inhabitants. However, most boaters are unaware or unsure of the short- and long-term detrimental effects that their presence has on harbor seals and other wildlife." My experience has been the same as Ms. Cowperthwaite's, and I have found her statement all too true of myself. I paddled for several years before I began to realize that my environmental ethics needed to be modified for sea kayaking. Assuming that people who take up a sport that is holistic and quiet already possess a certain level of care and knowledge about human impact on the environment, I begin my discussion by addressing particular situations and actions that specifically pertain to sea kayakers.

MINIMUM IMPACT WHILE ON LAND

The basic guidelines for minimum-impact camping and backpacking are applicable when you visit islands, with a few modifications. The guidelines also should be followed more strictly because islands' specialized ecologies are much more susceptible to catastrophe than most mainland areas.

VEGETATION: Island and beach plants must endure stressful conditions, much like an alpine environment, and are very fragile. Island soils are very thin and can take centuries to rebuild. Avoid stepping on any vegetation—walk on rocks or beaches as much as possible.

HUMAN WASTE: The most common impact from kayakers is human waste. For many years, I assumed that waste should be buried on the island in a six-inch-deep hole. The best method is, in fact, just the opposite. The thin, acidic soil on islands cannot break down wastes nearly as fast as the Atlantic ocean.

The *best* remedy is to carry out your waste in a plastic bag or Tupperware container. The next best method is to dispose of it in the ocean. There are a couple of ways to accomplish this. The first is the "shit-put." Deposit your waste on a nice flat, plate-sized rock, then hurl it out to sea. With practice, you can get the rock to land face-down, breaking the waste apart and helping it decompose even faster. Another method is to walk well away from your landing site (or where someone else might land) and do your thing as far as possible below the high-tide line. And of course, always pack out your toilet paper.

Be sure never to urinate in a tide pool, as this will drastically change the acid balance of the water, and many organisms will die before the tide flushes out the pool.

GARBAGE AND REFUSE: Everything should be packed off an island, including biodegradable material. As with human waste, food remnants decompose very slowly in island soils. An abandoned apple core may sit there for years.

Even better is to pack out more than you brought in. Stop on any beach, paddle any stretch of water, and you find bleach bottles, wrappers, pieces of rope, and the like. I carry a large garbage bag and make it a goal to fill it up before I come home. When I work with camps and educational groups, I make a game out of which boat can bring home the most trash. I'll never forget one pair of young men who found a large orange laundry basket which they strapped upright on the deck of their tandem. We spent the next three days shooting baskets with the trash we found.

The Maine Island Trail Association also sponsors clean-up days along the coast, including the Mount Desert area. Contact them for more information.

FIRES: The Maine Island Trail Association asks its members not to build any fires during July and August. If you do chose to build a fire, a permit is required from the Maine Forest Service on both private and state owned islands. Private islands additionally require the permission of the owner, and Acadia National Park forbids any fires on islands under its ownership.

Personally, I believe that islands and fires don't mix. Islands have limited soil nutrients; it could take well over a hundred years after a fire before an island can again support trees. You can survive three days without water, three weeks without food, and three lifetimes without fire. If you need heat, carry a stove.

LEAVING WHAT WE FIND: Acadia National Park recently published an article explaining how detrimental it can be to an environment if each visitor takes home a memento. Soon after, the park received a very heavy package from a woman who had been visiting the park for many years. Enclosed were a letter of apology and several years' worth of granite cobblestones. Please do not take anything but pleasant memories.

This is most important in terms of shell middens. These archaeological sites give us an irreplaceable history of past natural and social environments. As the *Maine Island Trail Guide* states: "Unscientific excavation of an archaeological site, such as searching for arrowheads or pottery bits for windowsill trinkets, is simple vandalism."

MINIMUM IMPACT ON THE WATER

It is easy to enjoy and learn about Mount Desert Island's environment while kayaking, without having a detrimental effect. In fact, our ultimate goal should be to have a positive impact. The key point to remember is that we are not the only boaters out on the water; there is a lobster boat ahead, a sailboat behind, and other kayakers in between.

CULTURAL IMPACT: When visiting any other culture (and goodness knows Maine is another culture) I try to be respectful. It is important to give way to working boats—particularly lobster and other fishing boats, ferries, and barges—since many people in coastal communities make their living as mariners. Minimize your time on boat ramps; others may be waiting to use them.

BIRDS: The general rule with birds—any type of bird—is to keep a good distance from them. If they take flight when I approach, I am too close. During the summer season when most people go paddling, birds are courting, building nests, mating, laying eggs, and raising their young. All in all, it's a pretty important time for birds. Disturbances can cause increased stress, lost food energy, and even the death of young chicks. Specific recommendations about individual bird species is given in the chapter "Marine Ecology."

MAMMALS: When they sight a seal or porpoise, many people react by paddling to where the animal just surfaced. Animals usually do not surface in the same place twice, so the eager paddler ends up sitting in the least likely place for the animal to reappear. It is, in fact, illegal to consciously paddle into a marine mammal's territory and cause it to leave or disrupt its feeding. That is considered "harassment" of the animal.

Instead, it's best to stop when you sight a seal or porpoise. This allows you a better chance of seeing the animal when it surfaces again. I have found that my sightings increase when I sit quiet and still in the water, as animals do not find my actions aggressive; sometimes they even approach me.

TWO CASE STUDIES

For seals and eagles, our behavior is critically important. In the case of the seals, the stress caused by kayakers appears to be unexpectedly high. Eagles are especially vulnerable to disturbance, because their population is so low.

KAYAKERS AND HARBOR SEALS

*Many of the paddlers . . . are so far away when the
seals first react to their presence that they never witness
the terror that runs through these animals. By the
time the paddlers arrive at the empty ledges, they never*

*suspect that they frightened the seals into the water
and placed great stress on the animals.*

Leslie Cowperthwaite

Based on her research, Leslie Cowperthwaite, of Maine Seal, has observed that harbor seals may tolerate disturbances by motorboats (often lobster boats) better than visitation by small unmotorized boats such as canoes or kayaks. Seals may stay hauled out in relaxed poses and even continue nursing their pups when motorboats pass by, but show a stress reaction when approached by small craft such as kayaks.

In the last few years, there has been a growing concern among the kayaking community and those researching harbor seals about why kayaks, in particular, seem to elicit panic. The reasons for this are not yet clear, but there is no question that paddlers should be aware of the issue and should make a point of not disturbing any seals that they see hauled out on ledges.

Being spooked from their haul-out sites is stressful for both mature and immature seals. They may not haul out again for up to twenty-four hours. Pups are forced to stop nursing, as they do so only on land, and with only a three- to four-week nursing period, this can be particularly detrimental. Not only are pups' energy stores depleted, but they must exert energy to thermoregulate, an underdeveloped ability in young seals. Mortality is high for pups permanently separated from their mothers, for adoption is rare. Adults are stressed if they are forced to enter the water, particularly during the molting season in July and August, when they need to stay in the sun while their metabolism works overtime during molting. There has also been documented abandonment by seals of their haul-out ledges due to human disturbance.

Since paddlers do run the risk of approaching these marine mammals too closely, we have a responsibility to plan our trips accordingly. In an effort to educate fellow kayakers, Leslie Cowperthwaite, together with Winston Shaw, a naturalist and director of the Coastal Maine Bald Eagle Project, wrote a paddler's etiquette toward seals, abbreviated by the acronym **PADDLE**:

Pass far—Avoid surprising seals hauled out on ledges and give them the widest berth possible. If you must pass ledges on which seals are hauled out, hug the shoreline farthest from the ledges, as this may allow you to "blend in."

APPROACH PARALLEL—Maintain a parallel course, as this is less threatening than a direct approach and allows the animals to see that you are merely passing by. Avoid changes in course or speed that might startle the seals.

DISCREET VIEWING—Restrain your impulse to get close to the seals. Do not engage in any activity that suggests that you are stalking the seals, such as pausing, taking photos, attempting to approach them undetected, etc. If you want to observe their natural, undisturbed behavior, do so from land (not from the seal ledges themselves) using binoculars or a spotting scope.

DEFER IMMEDIATELY—Back off immediately if the seals stretch their necks or chests higher into the air, or if they start to move toward the water, as this indicates they are preparing to flee. If the seals enter the water, leave the area immediately to avoid prolonging stress on the animals.

LEAVE ALONE—Do not handle or attempt to "rescue" seal pups apparently abandoned by their mothers. In most cases the mother and pup will reunite on their own. If you are concerned about a particular seal, contact the New England Aquarium at (917) 973-5247 or Allied Whale, College of the Atlantic, at (207) 288-5644.

EXPLAIN EFFECTS—Tell other sea kayakers and small boaters about the negative effects they can have on seals.

KAYAKERS AND BALD EAGLES

The recent effort to downlist bald eagles from "endangered" to "threatened" has brought particular attention to Maine eagles, which are still having a difficult time raising young (see page 127 in the "Marine Ecology" chapter).

The number-one factor harming eagles is contamination by pollutants such as DDT, dioxins, mercury, lead, and PCBs. While there is nothing we can do while kayaking to decrease these poisons, we can support research, educate others about eagles and toxins, and work to decrease the amount of poisons we use in other areas of our lives.

The second factor we can address directly. Studies have shown that eagles are very susceptible to human disturbance, and some will even move their nests to avoid human disturbance. Kayakers should follow some simple guidelines:

- Avoid paddling or landing near nests. Acadia National Park and the Maine Island Trail Association recommend staying at least one-half mile from nesting areas.
- Do not spend long amounts of time looking for or at nests. The more popular kayaking becomes, the more potential for disturbance, so each of us should keep our viewing time brief.
- If you see an eagle on land, do not paddle closer to the bird, causing it to take flight. Do not land on an island where you see an eagle perching.
- Avoid spending extended periods of time in known feeding territories. This can prevent the eagles from acquiring needed food energy for themselves and their young. Eagles often perch close to the shoreline near their feeding territories.
- Learn more about eagles, their habitat, and how you can help protect them.

CONCLUDING THOUGHTS

The first portion of this book offered guided journeys through the present; the next three chapters examined the past. In this final chapter, "Environmental Kayaking," I've addressed the future, which we all influence and create. Our paddling skills enable us to view wildlife, and the beauty of Acadia, as few others can. This is a gift and a special privilege.

I hope my guide inspires you to develop your own love for and connection to the Mount Desert region. My goals have been to impart an awareness of time and place and to promote respect for this area's natural history. By working to protect this unique resource, we can have a positive impact on its future.

Thank you, in advance.

> *Our task must be to free ourselves . . .*
> *by widening our circle of compassion to*
> *embrace all living creatures and the*
> *whole of nature and its beauty.*
>
> ALBERT EINSTEIN

Important Telephone Numbers

TELEPHONE NUMBERS IN ALL THE APPENDIXES ARE IN AREA CODE 207 UNLESS OTHERWISE SPECIFIED.

HOSPITALS

Mount Desert Island Hospital (Bar Harbor) • 288-5081

Northeast Harbor Medical Center • 276-3331

Southwest Harbor Community Health Center • 244-5630

POLICE

Bar Harbor emergency • 911
all other calls • 288-3391

Mount Desert • 276-5111

Southwest Harbor emergency • 244-5552;
all other calls • 244-7911

U.S. COAST GUARD

emergency • 244-5121
all other calls • 244-5517
VHF channel 16

HARBORMASTERS

Bar Harbor • 288-5571

Mount Desert • 276-5737

Southwest Harbor • 244-7913

ACADIA NATIONAL PARK

emergency • 288-3369
all other calls • 288-3338

ALLIED WHALE

288-5644

RED TIDE HOT LINE

entire Maine coast • 800-232-4733 OR 287-2099

Mount Desert Area • 667-3373

WEATHER FORECAST

667-8910

APPENDIX B

Helpful Information

HARDWARE/MARINE SUPPLY STORES

BAR HARBOR

Harbor Place • 288-3346

NORTHEAST HARBOR

F. T. Brown • 276-3329

SOUTHWEST HARBOR

Southwest Boat Marine Services • 244-5525

MANSET

Hinckley Ship Store • 244-7100

Manset Yacht Service • 244-4040

OUTDOOR RETAIL STORES

Cadillac Mountain Sports • 288-4532 (Bar Harbor)

OR 667-781 (Ellsworth)

L. L. Bean Factory Outlet • 865-4761 (Ellsworth)

MUSEUMS AND EDUCATIONAL RESOURCES

College of the Atlantic • 288-5015

Mount Desert Island Biological Laboratory • 288-3605

Jackson Laboratory • 288-3371

Mount Desert Oceanarium • 288-5005 (Bar Harbor)

OR 244-7330 (Southwest Harbor)

Abbe Museum • 288-2179

MAINE ENVIRONMENTAL ORGANIZATIONS

Island Institute • 594-9209

Maine Audubon Society • 781-2330

Maine Coast Heritage Trust • 276-5156

Natural Resources Council of Maine • 289-1110

The Nature Conservancy, Maine chapter • 729-5181

Maine Island Trail Association • 594-9209 or 761-8225

Friends of Acadia • 288-3340

Maine Bureau of Public Lands • 287-3061

Maine State Coastal Program • 287-3261
(ask about their publication called COASTLINKS:
A RESOURCE GUIDE TO MAINE'S COASTAL ORGANIZATIONS)

Maine Eagle Project, Maine Department of Inland
Fisheries and Wildlife • 941-4474

Equipment List

THIS SUGGESTED EQUIPMENT LIST IS FOR A DAY-PADDLE.

• Kayak, paddle with leash, spare paddle, spray skirt, life jacket (PFD), VHF radio or cell phone in waterproof radio bag, dry bags.

• Charts and chart bag, deck-mounted and handheld compass, tide chart, guidebook.

• Paddle float, stirrup sling, throw bag, towline, whistle, foghorn, flares and flare gun, bilge pump, sponge.

• First-aid kit, lunch plus emergency food, water plus extra two quarts, equipment-repair kit, duct tape.

• Paddling jacket and pants, pile or fleece shirt and pants, wool hat, socks, gloves, pogies (hand covers), appropriate footwear.

• Sun hat, sunglasses (with side shields), SPF 30 sunscreen and lip balm.

• OPTIONAL: Binoculars, camera, other field guides, journal or sketch-book, insect repellent.

Bibliography

THE FOLLOWING BOOKS HAVE BEEN HELPFUL TO ME IN EXPLORING AND LEARNING ABOUT THE MOUNT DESERT ISLAND AREA. THEY ARE LISTED BY SUBJECT. RELEVANT ORGANIZATIONS ARE ALSO INCLUDED.

KAYAKING SKILLS

Burch, David. *Fundamentals of Kayak Navigation, 2nd ed.* Chester, Conn.: Globe Pequot Press, 1993.
Study this book and you could probably get your captain's license. A necessity for any paddler's dry bag.

Dowd, John. *Sea Kayaking: A Manual for Long-distance Touring.* Seattle: Univ. of Washington Press, 1988.
Information on both short trips and longer expeditions based on Dowd's extensive career as a sea kayker.

Harrison, David. *Sea Kayaking Basics.* Fairfield, N. J.: Hearst Marine Books, 1993.
Despite its title, this book covers both basic and advanced skills.

Hutchinson, Derek. *Derek C. Hutchinson's Guide to Sea Kayaking.* Old Saybrook, Conn.: Globe Pequot Press, 1985
Thorough and well illustrated. Aimed at advanced paddlers but useful for all kayakers.

————. *Eskimo Rolling.* Camden, Me.: International Marine Publishing, 1988.
Good information for learning or perfecting your Eskimo roll.

Seidman, David. *The Essential Sea Kayaker: A Complete Course for the Open Water Traveler.* Camden, Me.: International Marine Publishing, 1992.
Written in an easy, accessible style, this book covers kayaking skills and overnight trips, including a chapter for disabled paddlers. Extensive bibliography.

Washburne, Randel. *The Coastal Kayaker's Manual: A Complete Guide to Skills, Gear, and Sea Sense, 2nd ed.* Old Saybrook, Conn.: Globe Pequot Press, 1989.
Another good manual covering basic skills.

A relatively new periodical, *Atlantic Coastal Kayaker,* is geared toward New England paddlers—a nice change from the many publications that focus only on the West Coast.

Cruising guides are also very helpful for local information. I prefer the following two:

Taft, Hank, and Jan Taft. *A Cruising Guide to the Maine Coast, 3rd edition.* Peaks Island, Me.: Diamond Press, 1996.

Duncan, Roger, and John Ware. *A Cruising Guide to the New England Coast, Including the Hudson River, Long Island Sound, and the Coast of New Brunswick.* New York: G. P. Putnam's Sons, 1990.

GEOLOGY

Chapman, C. A. *The Geology of Acadia National Park.* Old Greenwich, Conn.: Chatham Press, 1970.
Excellent explanation of the geological processes that formed the Mount Desert Island area. The information is a bit technical, but fine for the layperson. It includes guided geology trips to take by car and on foot. Highly recommended.

Gilman, R.; C. Chapman; T. Lowell; and H. Borns. *The Geology of Mount Desert Island: A Visitor's Guide to the Geology of Acadia National Park.* Maine Geology Survey, Department of Conservation, 1988.
Easily understood explanation of bedrock formation and glaciation. Good illustrations, including two excellent bedrock and surface geology maps of Mount Desert Island.

Johnson, Douglas. *The New England–Acadian Shoreline.*
New York: John Wiley and Sons, Inc., 1925.
Technical and thick, with some information on Mount Desert Island.

Kendall, David. *Glaciers and Granite: A Guide to Maine's
Landscape and Geology.* Camden Me.: Down East Books,
1987. *Reprinted by North Country Press, Belfast, Me.*
*Good description of Maine geology, with information on the coast,
mountains, water, plate tectonics, and the interaction between humans
and geology. Includes descriptions of features along major roads in Maine.*

Raisz, E. *The Scenery of Mount Desert Island:
Its Origin and Development.* Annals of the New York
Academy of Sciences, v. 31 (1929), 121–86.
*Although written in 1929, this technical book is still useful and
informative for geology buffs.*

ECOLOGY

Amos, William, and Steven Amos. *Atlantic and Gulf Coasts.*
New York: Alfred A. Knopf, Inc., 1985
*One of my favorites. Good photos and some information about
organisms, habitats, and ecosystems. When I can only bring one
field guide, this is the one.*

Bayer, Robert, and Juanita Bayer. *Lobsters Inside-out:
A Guide to the Maine Lobster.* Bar Harbor, Me.:
Acadia Press, 1989.
A childrens' book completely devoted to lobsters.

Boehmer, Raquel. *A Foraging Vacation, Edibles from Maine's
Sea and Shore.* Camden, Me.: Down East Books, 1982.
*Useful information on gathering and using wild foods, including
recipes. Good for beginners.*

Borrill, Michael, and Deborah Borrill. *A Sierra Club Naturalist's Guide to the North Atlantic Coast, Cape Cod to
Newfoundland.* San Francisco: Sierra Club Books, 1981.
*Good complement to a field guide, with a strong emphasis on
the environment.*

Butcher, Russell. *Field Guide to Acadia National Park,
Maine.* New York: Reader's Digest Press, 1977.
*Information on sea and shore plants, animals, and rocks.
Also includes guided hikes.*

Katona, Steven; Valerie Rough; and David Richardson. *A Field Guide to Whales, Porpoises, and Seals from Cape Cod to Newfoundland, 4th rev. ed.* Washington, D. C.: Smithsonian Institution Press, 1993.
Written for layperson and expert alike, this guide gives up-to-date information on many species. Numerous photographs and drawings.

Kingsbury, John. *The Rocky Shore.* Old Greenwich, Conn.: Chatham Press, Inc., 1970.
User-friendly, expertly illustrated children's book with good introduction to the tidal zone. Written by a professor of botany. Strong emphasis on ecology and the environment.

Livingston, Susan; Charles Todd, William Krohn, and Ray Owen. "Habitat Models for Nesting Bald Eagles in Maine." *Journal of Wildlife Management* 54, 4 (1990), 644–53.
Excellent information on Maine's eagle population.

Long, Ralph. *Native Birds of Mount Desert Island and Acadia National Park.* Mount Desert Island, Me.: Beech Hill Publishing Co., 1982.
An updated version of the work of a local naturalist who knew and loved the birds in this area. Brief descriptions and sighting locations of all local birds.

Miller, Dorcas. *The Maine Coast: A Nature Lover's Guide.* Charlotte, N. C.: East Wood Press, Maine Audubon Society, 1979.
Excellent descriptions of history, wildlife, and ecosystems; discussion of activities and organizations; good bibliography.

Robbins, Sarah, and Clarice Yentsch. *The Sea Is All about Us; A Guidebook to the Marine Environments of Cape Ann and Other Northern New England Waters.* Salem, Mass.: Peabody Essex Museum, 1973.
Descriptions of marine organisms and environmental conditions that affect marine life.

Another source of information on coastal ecology is the Critical Areas Program of the Maine State Planning Office, which has published a series of pamphlets on various animals and habitats within Maine's Critical Areas Program.

SOCIAL HISTORY

Binnewies, Esther, and Muriel Davisson. *History of Bartlett's Island, Mount Desert. Me.* Portland, Me.: Seavey Printers, 1981.

Caldwell, Bill. *Islands of Maine: Where America Really Began.* Portland, Me.: Guy Gannett Publishing Co., 1981.
The bible of historical facts. Excellent explanations, including information not commonly known.

Conkling, Philip. *Islands in Time, A Natural and Human History of the Islands of Maine.* Camden, Me.: Down East Books, 1981.
Written by an expert on Maine islands and ecology, this is the best commentary on the connection between the natural and human histories of the Maine coast. Highly recommended.

Hale, Richard. *The Story of Bar Harbor: An Informal History Recording One Hundred and Fifty Years in the Life of a Community.* New York: Ives Washburn, Inc, 1949.
Very detailed history of Bar Harbor.

Harmon, Kathryn. "**The Treasures of Old Farm: The Story of George Dorr's Family Home at Compass Harbor and the Artifacts that Outlived It.**" Unpublished senior thesis, College of the Atlantic, Bar Harbor, Me, 1994.
A wonderful history with pictures and maps of this historic house. Available at the College of the Atlantic library.

Helfrich, G. W. and Gladys O'Neil. *Lost Bar Harbor.* Camden Me.: Down East Books, 1982.
History of Bar Harbor's rusticator mansions and hotels, with many photographs.

McLane, Charles. *Islands of the Mid-Maine Coast: Blue Hill Bay.* Woolwich, Me.: Kennebec River Press, Inc., 1985.
This bible of island life traces each family member and resident of the islands of Blue Hill Bay. Extensive information on economy and lifestyle.

———. *Islands of the Mid-Maine Coast: Mount Desert to Machias Bay.* Falmouth, Me.: Kennebec River Press, 1989.
Using the same format as in his book on Blue Hill Bay, McLane in this

account includes Bartlett Narrows, Frenchman Bay, Somes Sound, and islands south of Mount Desert.

Rich, Louise Dickinson. *The Coast of Maine, An Informal History and Guide.* Cornwall N.Y.: Cornwall Press, Inc., 1962. Reprinted by Down East Books, Camden, Me.,1993.
Informative and well-written history of the coast.

St. Germain, Tom, and Jay Saunders. *Trails of History: The Story of Mount Desert Island's Paths from Norumbega to Acadia.* Bar Harbor, Me.: Parkman Publications, 1993.
Well-written and interesting. A perfect companion for trips ashore.

Simpson, Dorothy. *The Maine Islands in Story and Legend.* Nobleboro, Me.: Blackberry Books, 1987.
Includes brief histories of Swan's Island, Bartlett's Island (outdated), Mount Desert, and the Cranberry Islands. Also discusses the Maine Seacoast Mission.

Wilmerding, John. *The Artist's Mount Desert: American Painters on the Maine Coast.* Princeton, N. J.: Princeton Univ. Press, 1994.
Tells about the artists who came to Mount Desert in the mid- to late 1800s. Many illustrations.

Young, Hazel. *Islands of New England.* Boston: Little, Brown and Company, 1954.
Good accounts of islanders' mentality, the Maine Seacoast Mission, Mount Desert Island, and the Cranberry Islands.

Another source of information about the social history of islands is the *Island Journal*. Published by the Island Institute (Rockland, Maine), this annual magazine contains well-written articles on many aspects of island life.

ENVIRONMENTAL KAYAKING

Amato, Chris. "**A Sense of Balance: Working toward a New Wildlife Ethic for Kayakers.**" *Sea Kayaker* (December 1995), 37–41.

Dillon, Forrest. "**How to Minimize Our Impact on Seals.**" *Atlantic Coastal Kayaker* (April 1994), 11–12.

Hill, Ruth Ann. "Seal Watch: Enjoying the Maine Coast's Most Popular Marine Mammals." *Maine Boats and Harbors* 30 (June/July 1994), 31–36.

Jacobi, Charles. "Bald Eagle Management Plan." Acadia National Park, 1994.

McCullough, Gale. "Seals and Sea Kayakers." *Atlantic Coastal Kayaker* (April 1994), 1–11.

Read, Andrew; Scott Kraus; Kathryn Bisack; and Debra Palka. "Harbor Porpoises and Gill Nets in the Gulf of Maine." *Conservation Biology* 7 (1993), 189–93.

Shaw, Winston, "Seals and Sea Kayakers: Taking a Look at Myth." *Sea Kayaker* (Spring 1991), 14–17.

Index